LINCOLN'S WARTIME TOURS
from
WASHINGTON, D.C.

LINCOLN'S WARTIME TOURS
— *from* —
WASHINGTON, D.C.

JOHN W. SCHILDT

THE
History
PRESS

Published by The History Press
Charleston, SC
www.historypress.com

Copyright © 2020 by John W. Schildt

Originally printed 2010. The History Press edition 2020.

Cover images courtesy of the Library of Congress.

First published 2020

Manufactured in the United States

ISBN 9781467145718

Library of Congress Control Number: 2020932099

To Miss Edith Nicodemus, the first-grade teacher at Walkersville Elementary School, who initially told me about Mr. Lincoln. Also, to Judge Edward S. Delaplaine, a writer and historian who befriended and encouraged the author.

CONTENTS

CONTENTS

ACKNOWLEDGEMENTS

With gratitude to Miss Edith Nicodemus, a first-grade teacher who awakened a love of Mr. Lincoln;

Judge Edward S. Delaplaine, a Lincoln scholar who was a source of constant encouragement;

John Frye, a walking encyclopedia of knowledge about the roads and countryside in southern Washington County;

Dennis Frye, author, historian, preservationist and friend who shared his knowledge on the Showman farms, the headquarters of Ambrose Burnside and George B. McClellan at Antietam;

John Hennessy, author and historian who furnished a wealth of material about Lincoln's visit to the Army of the Potomac in the spring of 1863;

Edward Itnrye, a gentleman who discovered Lincoln's route from Antietam to Frederick;

Colonel Jerry Meyers, who took photos and did research for me on Aquia Creek;

Frank O'Reilly, historian and author who shared information on the Fredericksburg area;

Alann Schmidt, ranger historian at Antietam who provided archival assistance;

Ted Alexander, formerly chief historian at Antietam, who asked the writer to give a lecture on Lincoln's travels for one of his seminars—the lecture led to the book;

Chris Vincent, chief guide at Antietam, and fellow guides Jim Buchanan and Bill Sagle for their assistance with the images;

And Kate Jenkins of The History Press for her expertise and guidance in bringing this work to fruition.

To all of these, we say, "Thank you!" Without your assistance, this work could not have been accomplished.

INTRODUCTION

On a February morning, a group of first graders at Walkersville Elementary School waited for class to begin. It was Abraham Lincoln's birthday.

When class began, Miss Edith Nicodemus, the teacher, had many objects to share with us. There was a miniature log cabin, a small fence rail and a picture of Lincoln stretched out before the fireplace reading the Bible, as well as various other pictures of Lincoln. Her presentation awakened a spark in me—an interest in people and places, as well as in Mr. Lincoln. Miss Edith also gave each of us a shiny new penny. I still have mine.

Early in my teenage years, I timidly approached one of Maryland's foremost historians and writers, the Honorable Edward S. Delaplaine, a prominent jurist. Judge Delaplaine had written on Francis Scott Key, John Philip Sousa and a host of other subjects. He also gave me a copy of *Fighting for Time*, the story of the Battle of Monocacy. Judge Glenn S. Worthington was one of his contemporaries. Judge Delaplaine had also completed what I believe to be the first work on Lincoln's visit to Antietam, in a brief called *Lincoln and His Traveling Companions to Antietam*.

Judge Delaplaine gladly shared his research and constantly befriended and encouraged the author. It is for this reason this book is dedicated to Miss Edith and to Judge Delaplaine. They lit the spark, and to them I shall be eternally grateful.

A TRAVELING MAN

Today, the President of the United States travels long distances on Air Force One. For short journeys, he flies on a Marine Corps helicopter. The President travels first class, with bulletproof limousines for ground travel. Advance people check out security, and in parades or other gatherings, members of the Secret Service are everywhere. Such was not the case during the years between 1861 and 1865, when Abraham Lincoln was the sixteenth President of the United States.

As a boy, Lincoln traveled on foot, horseback, flatboat and Conestoga wagon. As a lawyer, he rode his Illinois judicial circuit traveling by horseback. To the end of his life, he knew and admired good horses.

Today, jet travel is the primary method of transportation. In the day of Mr. Lincoln, the train was king. One of the great moments of Lincoln's life occurred on February 11, 1861, as he prepared to leave his Springfield home for Washington. He walked out the door of his home and closed it, never to return. And as his friends and neighbors gathered in the rain, Mr. Lincoln bade them farewell.[1]

The cold drizzle brought numbness to Lincoln and his party of fifteen as they approached the Great Western Station. The gray mist of the dawn seemed more indicative of twilight. The locomotive was already puffing steam. Behind the engine were a baggage car and a special passenger car. The president and the superintendent of the Great Western were awaiting Mr. Lincoln. One thousand people had gathered at the little brick station to see Mr. Lincoln off.

A path was cleared from the station to the car. As Lincoln walked among them, hands were stretched out for one last touch from one of their own.

Apparently, he had not intended to make a speech. Mr. Lincoln did not like to make impromptu speeches. He always wanted to be prepared and have some notes. But as he reached the platform of the car, he took off his hat. He looked out over the crowd. He saw his friends and neighbors of many years. His heart was filled with great emotion. He looked almost like he was standing by a grave site. The members of the crowd took off their hats, almost as if in salute. Then Mr. Lincoln spoke:

> *Friends, no one who has never been placed in a like position can understand my feelings at this hour nor the impressive sadness I feel at this parting. For more than a quarter of a century I have lived among you, and during all that time I have received nothing but kindness at your hands. Here I have lived from my youth till now I am an old man. Here the most sacred trusts of earth were assumed; here all my children were born and one of them lies buried. To you, dear friends, I owe all that I have, all that I am. All the strange checkered past seems to crowd now upon my mind. Today I leave you; I go to assume a task more difficult than that which devolved upon General Washington. Unless the great God who assisted him shall be with and aid me, I must fail. But if the same omniscient mind and the same Almighty arm that directed and protected him shall guide and support me, I shall not fail; I shall succeed. Let us all pray that the God of our fathers may not forsake us now. To Him I commend you all. Permit me to ask that with equal sincerity and faith you will all invoke His wisdom and guidance for me. With these few words I must leave you—for how long I know not. Friends, one and all, I must now bid you an affectionate farewell.*

This speech is indicative of the life and character of Lincoln and is symbolic of his approach to his wartime travels. Had Lincoln not given his famed Gettysburg Address or the Second Inaugural, his Farewell Address at Springfield, given to his friends and neighbors, would have ensured his place in the realms of great literature.

Then, it was time to go. Lincoln surveyed the crowd and gazed over Springfield. It was his last look. He would never return. The engine began to puff as more coal was added to the boiler. The wheels began to turn, slowly, then faster, and in the gray dawn, Mr. Lincoln began his journey to greatness.[2]

During the following days, Lincoln visited key cities, met with five governors and made twenty speeches. Military units met the President elect at each stop. The Wabash train arrived in Indianapolis, and Lincoln was met by Governor Oliver P. Morton. From the balcony of the Bates House, he advocated silence instead of inflammatory rhetoric.

On his fifty-second birthday, Lincoln stopped in Cincinnati for more speeches and another parade. He made a good impression on the city's large German element. Then a special train carried Mr. Lincoln to Columbus. In the Ohio capital, he spoke of the great burden that had fallen on him, one greater than that of George Washington.

The next stop was Pittsburgh. Once again, there was "a flattering reception." Then it was on to Cleveland and a two-mile procession through rain and mud. In Buffalo, New York, the surge of the crowd was so great that in an effort to protect Lincoln, Major David Hunter had his collarbone dislocated. Stops were also made in Rochester, Syracuse and Utica.[3]

In Albany, Lincoln expressed the hope that he could speak for the good of the country, both the North and the South. The train headed south along the banks of the Hudson River to New York City. He had received thirty-five thousand votes in the city. A procession of thirty carriages awaited him. It took five hundred policemen to handle the crowd at the Astor House. Lincoln rode to the Astor in a carriage that had transported the Prince of Wales a short time before. A southerner wore black kid gloves instead of the formal white ones dictated by the occasion. The reason: "I think we should send some flowers to…the Undertaker of the Union." Tad and Willie went to a play and also to P.T. Barnum's Museum.

In Trenton, New Jersey, Lincoln spoke of the importance of his task: "If [the ship of state] should suffer attack now, there will be no pilot ever needed for another voyage."

Then it was on to Philadelphia. Lincoln stood for two hours shaking hands and greeting well-wishers. Then he received a visitor with disturbing news. It was Allan Pinkerton, a railroad detective on duty with the Philadelphia, Wilmington and Baltimore Railroad. He had been called to duty because there were fears that southerners might try to derail trains or destroy bridges and roadbeds. Pinkerton related that he had received news of a threat and plot to assassinate Mr. Lincoln in Baltimore. Lincoln listened politely but refused to change his plans. He was to give a speech at Independence Hall in the morning. The speech would be given, and then he would go to Harrisburg. After that, he would consider the plot against his life. During the night, Frederick Seward, the son of Lincoln's announced secretary of state, arrived. He carried an important message from his father—Seward had also heard of the plot against Lincoln.

But morning came, and Lincoln raised the flag at Independence Hall on the birthday of George Washington. There was applause and cheering as the announcement was made of the admission of Kansas to the Union of the United States. Lincoln, in brief remarks, stated that he saw "no need of bloodshed and war." Later, he spoke in Harrisburg and stated that he would lean on the people for support. He made several speeches in Harrisburg and conferred with Andrew Curtin, governor of Pennsylvania.

To meet the threat against Lincoln's life, the train left early and arrived in Baltimore around 3:30 a.m.; then, after a change of trains, it proceeded to Washington, which was reached at 6:00 a.m. Abraham Lincoln, who would shortly be inaugurated as the sixteenth president of the United States, had arrived in the nation's capital. It was February 24. Pinkerton and others may have saved Lincoln's life. However, from the moment of the threat, whether real or imagined, from then on, Lincoln was daily under the cloud of a possible violent act.

Mr. Lincoln was in Washington, a great task set upon him, that of endeavoring to keep the Union together and prevent war. He sent his Illinois friend Ward Hill Lamon to the South in an effort to avert war. However, the situation had gone too far, and on April 12, 1861, shells fell on Fort Sumter. The War Between the States, the American Civil War, had begun.

In the North and South, there were torchlight parades. Fiery speeches were delivered. The states and wealthy individuals sought to raise troops. There was almost a carnival air, with little realization of the cost and the human suffering that was to follow. Mr. Lincoln called for seventy-five thousand volunteers to put down the rebellion, causing Virginia to secede. It was a dark time.

Many felt that the war would end with one dramatic battle. And on Sunday, July 21, 1861, the First Battle of Bull Run or Manassas was fought west of Washington. It was a disaster for the Union cause. The Union and the Confederacy, and therefore the generals, settled in for a long war and the building of armies. During 1861, Mr. Lincoln remained in Washington. But then, in 1862, he began his wartime travels.

Mr. Lincoln made nineteen wartime trips from Washington to other destinations. Thirteen of the journeys went south to Virginia. Three times Lincoln ventured into Maryland, twice into Pennsylvania and one trip to New York State. Most of the travels were military in nature. Lincoln ventured from the confines of Washington for three primary reasons:

- To confer with his generals.
- To plot military strategy.
- To visit the troops in the field.

Twice, on travels to Baltimore and Philadelphia, Lincoln journeyed to make appearances at Sanitary Fairs. These were attempts by the Sanitary Commission to raise funds and materials for the sick and wounded soldiers. They were similar to Red Cross efforts today.

Lincoln's primary means of wartime travel was by train. Several times he sailed down the Potomac River and the Chesapeake Bay to reach Fort Monroe or City Point. The naval vessel often served as Presidential quarters. Lincoln then went ashore via a smaller boat, taking a train and then often riding horseback to confer with generals and visit troops.

The travels were not without incident. On one expedition, the naval vessel had to put into a cove near Indian Head, Maryland, to ride out a storm. A snowstorm had struck in early April 1863 and caused choppy seas. Today, the Secret Service would be greatly alarmed about such a situation. Another time, a team of horses bolted as Mr. Lincoln, returning from a Virginia trip, prepared to take a carriage from the Navy Yard back to the White House. Then there were the histrionics of Mary Todd Lincoln during the President's last journey in March and April 1865. She flew into a rage because first the wife of General Griffin and then the wife of General Ord were near Mr. Lincoln, occupying a position Mary thought should have been reserved for the wife of the President. She even berated Julia Grant, suggesting that she had her eyes on the White House. This caused great embarrassment for Mr. Lincoln. Many who witnessed these episodes looked upon Mary Lincoln as "a sick woman."

There is another interesting note. Although the trips provided Mr. Lincoln an escape from the rigors of the White House office and afforded him the opportunity to mingle with the men in the ranks, he often suffered poor health prior to, during or just after his wartime travels. The most common problem was a stomach ailment. Often there were cramps and discomfort. On one trip, the President attributed the problem to bad water. The steamer stopped at Fort Monroe for a supply of fresh water.

Prior to the Gettysburg trip, the problem was parental and emotional. On November 18, 1863, Lincoln was sad and depressed because Tad was too ill to eat. And there were prevailing problems—Mrs. Lincoln was again distraught.

After Gettysburg, Lincoln had another ailment. A note for November 21, 1863, stated, "President Lincoln ill with a mild case of smallpox."

However, he maintained his sense of humor by saying, "Now I have something I can give to everybody."[4]

More than half of Lincoln's wartime travels were to Virginia—nine were taken in 1862, and seven of those were to Virginia. The other two were to West Point in June and then to Harpers Ferry and Antietam in October.

Five trips were taken in 1863. The first three were to Falmouth, Virginia, to confer with General Joseph Hooker. Then there was the famous Gettysburg trip in November, and just after Christmas, Mr. Lincoln visited the large Confederate prison at Point Lookout, Maryland.

There were four trips in 1864; two were military in nature, and for the other two, Lincoln appeared at the Sanitary Fairs assisting in the effort to support the health needs of Union soldiers.

His time in 1865 was short, but in February Mr. Lincoln sailed to Hampton Roads to confer with the Confederate Peace Commissioners, and then nearly two weeks were spent at City Point, conferring with U.S. Grant, William T. Sherman and others, as well as visiting the troops as they took part in the final actions of the war.

History is people and places. In the pages of this book, we shall look at the people and places Lincoln visited during these years. We'll consider where he stayed, what he said and what he did on his wartime travels.

For some of his travels, there is little information. The White House and the presidency were not covered as closely in 1862 as they are now. Likewise, some of the trips were made in secret.

The Gettysburg Address has been the subject of various books, so that section is a mere summation of the great event. The trips to Antietam in 1862 and the visit to Hooker's army in the spring of 1863 are covered at length. The visit to City Point at the end of the war, and near the end of his life, was Lincoln's longest journey, two weeks in length. Thus it is the largest section. The book seeks to present an overview of Lincoln's wartime travels.

TRAVELS IN 1862

President Lincoln made his wartime travels by train or ship. The Northern journeys were primarily by train, usually the Baltimore and Ohio. The many trips to Virginia were by boat. There were four primary routes into Virginia. These were by way of the Shenandoah Valley or a thrust on Richmond by way of Manassas or Fredericksburg. These routes were impractical because Confederate armies controlled the overland route. The other two routes were by sea. The Union navy controlled the water approaches. One was south on the Potomac River to Aquia Creek and then by land to Fredericksburg—this was the shortest route to Richmond. The other, a longer route, was also by the Potomac River and then to the Chesapeake Bay, sticking close to the coastline to Fort Monroe, and finally the York and James Rivers. Eventually, the Army of the Potomac used both water routes to move large numbers of troops, plus tons of supplies to its bases of operation.

The launching point for the Virginia trips was the U.S. Naval Yard. It was a bustling place employing nearly two thousand workers. They worked in shifts to turn out chains for cables, boilers for the ships, naval gun carriages and cannons, anchors and other naval items. They also repaired and refitted ships.[5]

When the President headed south to visit the troops and confer with the leaders of the armies, he came to the Navy Yard and usually took a small, fast steamer to Aquia Creek, City Point or Fort Monroe. The *River Queen* seems to have been his favorite.

The year 1862 was a crucial one for Mr. Lincoln as an individual and as the chief executive. The war had not ended quickly, the Southern states were still in rebellion and for most of the year, with the exception of U.S. Grant in the west, he was plagued with the problem of military leadership. Lincoln was caught in the middle in a tug of war among radical, moderate and conservative politicians and generals. The nation had never faced such problems before. There were growing pains, war and suffering. Therefore, it is not surprising that Lincoln made nine wartime travels in 1862.

As a sidelight, he made a short jaunt prior to visiting his commanders and troops in the field. On April 1, 1862, he went to Alexandria to confer with General McClellan prior to his departure to Old Point Comfort, Virginia. McClellan had hopes of advancing on the peninsula between the York and James Rivers and threatening Richmond.

The next day, April 3, the President, Mrs. Lincoln and their sons, accompanied by Commander John Dahlgren, sailed down the Potomac to visit Mount Vernon, the home of President George Washington. While the family visited the estate, Lincoln remained on board the steamer.[6]

On April 19, 1862, Mr. Lincoln, accompanied by Secretaries Stanton and Chase, Commander Dahlgren and D. Dudley Field, a New York merchant, traveled to the Washington Navy Yard. There the group boarded the revenue cutter *Miami* for a trip down the Potomac to confer with Major General Irvin McDowell.[7]

The Union general had some impressive credentials. He had studied in France and then graduated from the U.S. Military Academy, class of 1838. He stood twenty-third in a class of forty-five. McDowell served on the frontier and then in the Mexican-American War and then became an instructor in tactics at West Point. This was the typical prewar military routine. McDowell was then assigned to army headquarters in Washington and through Winfield Scott met Lincoln. In 1861, he was given command of Union troops south of the Potomac. Washington politicians urged him to do battle, and he did so reluctantly, feeling that his troops were not yet ready for combat. The result was the disaster at the First Battle of Bull Run. In April 1862, McDowell was commanding the Army of the Rappahannock.

For some reason, McDowell did not arrive for the meeting. Therefore, Lincoln and the rest of the party spent the night on board the *Miami*. McDowell did arrive very early on the morning of April 20 and accompanied the President on the trip back to Washington. The *Miami* arrived at about 2:30 p.m. Lincoln dined at the home of Commander Dahlgren.

The naval officer Dahlgren was the son of the Swedish consul at Philadelphia. He attended the U.S. Naval Academy. For sixteen years, he served as ordnance officer. It was during this time that he invented the Dahlgren gun, a rifled cannon, as well as boat howitzers with iron carriages. Early in the war, he was in charge of Union naval ordnance and later commanded the South Atlantic Blockading Squadron. He was also the father of Ulric Dahlgren, who served in his early twenties on the staffs of Franz Sigel, Ambrose Burnside and Joseph Hooker. Young Dahlgren was badly wounded in the streets of Hagerstown during the retreat from Gettysburg and lost his leg.

The trip to Aquia was the first of Lincoln's wartime travels. Perhaps symbolic of future trips, Lincoln had a major problem getting from the Navy Yard to the White House. The team of excited horses bolted, immobilizing the Presidential carriage. Another rig and team had to be obtained.[8]

Shortly, Mr. Lincoln would be sailing again, this time to Fort Monroe. A long point of land commands the passageway leading from the Chesapeake Bay to Hampton Roads. Ships had to pass the point on their travels proceeding on the James River to Richmond or on the Elizabeth River to Norfolk. Standing majestically on the high ground is the "Gibraltar of North America," Fort Monroe.

Military experts, realizing the strategic location, began erecting defenses as early as 1819. In 1831, a young engineer officer by the name of Robert E. Lee arrived on the scene. A garrison was already stationed at the fort, used as an artillery training school. However, the outer works still had to be constructed, and there was also a plan to place another fort offshore. This was to be constructed by sinking rocks into the water.[9]

Robert E Lee married while assigned to Fort Monroe. One month later, he brought his bride, Mary Anna Custis, to the fort. The young couple took residence in the Talcott House. Mary felt confined. After all, she had been accustomed to the vastness of Arlington House. She was also disturbed by the rowdiness of the garrison. There was a lot of drunkenness.

Alarm spread through the area in 1831. Nat Turner fomented a rebellion that led to the deaths of 55 persons. This was in South Hampton County, fifty miles from the fort. As a result, the garrison was strengthened to 680 men. This was 10 percent of the U.S. Army at the time. The army had reached its lowest point.

In 1832, the first son of Robert and Mary Anna Lee was born at Fort Monroe. Born on September 16, the boy was named George Washington Custis Lee. Joining the officer corps on the post was a young man by the name of Joseph E. Johnston.[10]

Much of Lee's time was devoted to the construction of what was called at the time Fort Calhoun, being built on the riprap offshore. It was later called Fort Wool.

During the winter of 1862, with suggestions from General William B. Franklin, General McClellan devised his Urbanna Plan, calling for an amphibious attack on Richmond. In a twenty-two-page proposal, McClellan agreed that the transportation and supply problems might be difficult, although the Urbanna Plan had advantages over moving on Manassas. It took Lincoln a while to agree to the plan. Secretary Stanton tried to prod McClellan to action. He wrote to the *New York Tribune*, "Battles are to be won…by boldly pursuing and striking the enemy."

In the midst of all this, a pall of gloom fell over the White House. On February 20, Willie, the eleven-year-old son of President and Mrs. Lincoln, passed away. The first family was devastated, but the affairs of state had to continue.

Lincoln and the War Department approved the Urbanna Plan with certain conditions. Among them, Washington of course had to be adequately defended, and the Army of the Potomac had to begin moving within ten days.

However, the Confederates had devised an ironclad ship, the *Merrimack*, to threaten Union vessels. This necessitated some changes. McClellan now planned to sail down to Fort Monroe. The historic old fort would serve as a secure base of operations.

Midway between Richmond and Washington is Fredericksburg. In the Civil War, it had the misfortune of being on the main road between the two cities and thus, until 1864, the target of the Union advances on Richmond.

Fredericksburg is steeped in American history. As early as 1608, John Smith ventured to the falls of the Rappahannock exploring the inland wilderness. By 1727, a town had been established on the south bank of the river. The town was officially chartered in that year. It was named for Frederick, Prince of Wales. The streets were named after the royal House of Hanover. After the Revolutionary War, additional streets were named after prominent figures from the conflict.

In 1738, Augustine Washington purchased the Ferry Farm on the north shore of the Rappahannock. This is considered the boyhood home of George Washington. For several years after he grew to manhood, he represented Fredericksburg in the Virginia House of Burgesses. He also purchased a home for his mother, Mary, in 1772. She lived in the house until her death in 1789. A sister, Betty, married Fielding Lewis, a wealthy planter, and moved to the lovely plantation home known as Kenmore.

James Monroe brought his bride to Fredericksburg in 1789 and began his law practice there. Thomas Jefferson met with other prominent Virginians to draft, in 1777, the Virginia Statute of Religious Freedom. This became the basis for the First Amendment to the Constitution.

During the War Between the States, Fredericksburg suffered greatly. It was shelled by Union artillery, and much of the town was destroyed. The homes were looted by Union soldiers. The area became a hospital after the disaster on Marye's Heights, and many of the civilians became refugees.

With things going well on the peninsula for George McClellan and the Army of the Potomac, Lincoln turned his attention on Fredericksburg and the troops under Irvin McDowell. He longed for a two-pronged offensive. Maybe McClellan and McDowell could crush the Confederacy.

From the tip of the historic peninsula between the York and James Rivers, McClellan and his huge army consisting of four corps would move on Richmond. Actually, the distance from Fort Monroe to Richmond was seventy miles, ten miles less than the distance from Manassas to Richmond.

Four hundred ships were amassed to transport 121,000 men, nearly 15,000 animals and all the other military equipment to Fort Monroe. It was a tremendous undertaking. Some have said it was the 1862 equivalent to the D-Day armada. For the next month, the Army of the Potomac would operate on the peninsula fifty miles long and fifteen miles wide. McClellan's plan had the possibility of success. However, he exhibited that which was to become his trademark: "the slows." His tardiness gave the Confederates the opportunity to send reinforcements and to entrench. On May 6, McClellan won a victory at the Battle of Williamsburg. Now Richmond was just fifty miles away.

The previous day, Mr. Lincoln had sailed for Fort Monroe to "see what was taking McClellan so long." He wanted to infuse some vigor into the army and navy. Prior to his departure, Lincoln conversed with Samuel Strong, the inventor of the breechloading carbine. At about dusk, Lincoln sailed on the *Miami*. For some reason, they spent the night fifteen miles south of Alexandria and resumed the journey the next morning.

Lincoln as a wartime president sought to devise some military strategy. Along with Secretary of War Stanton and Secretary Chase, he proposed to take Norfolk, the home base of the *Merrimack*. The evacuation of Yorktown had left Norfolk exposed. With the assistance of the Union navy and ten thousand troops stationed at Fort Monroe, Lincoln and Stanton wanted to capture Norfolk and deny the *Merrimack* a base of operations.

After his arrival, Lincoln conferred briefly with officer Louis Goldsborough of the U.S. Navy, as well as with Major General John Wool, the commander of Fort Monroe. Wool was seventy-eight years old and a veteran of the War of 1812. However, he was still very sharp. Lincoln spent the night on the *Miami*, and in the morning, he boarded the naval flagship, the *Minnesota*. With his tall hat and cape, he looked like a figure from a comic opera, ready to sail for the California gold fields.

On May 8, Lincoln ordered a flotilla of Federal ships, led by the *Monitor*, to bombard Confederate positions at Sewell's Point, located seven and a half miles north of Norfolk. After the bombardment, troops were to land.

However, the CSA *Virginia*, or the *Merrimack*, steamed up to confront the invaders. The transports and ships turned. A safer place and a site where the Virginia was unlikely to venture was selected. Lincoln, Stanton and Chase stood on the ramparts to watch the bombardment. Later, he boarded a tugboat and observed the continued shelling of Sewell's Point and Craney Island.

On May 9, the President took a cruise around Hampton Roads on the *Miami*. Then he held a conference with General Wool and others at Fort Monroe. The decision was made to send troops against Norfolk. The strategy session continued over the lunch hour. General Wool remarked, "If you stay here, 8 hours, I will present Norfolk to you." Shortly after lunch, the President became a military man. He and Secretary Stanton looked for possible landing places for the proposed march on Norfolk. They rode around in a tugboat.

At about 2:00 p.m., the President went to a site about one mile below Fort Wool. Lincoln went ashore and the troops embarked.

The following day, Lincoln, along with Secretaries Chase and Stanton, accompanied General Wool to the landing point for the march on Norfolk, Willoughby Point. Secretary Chase went with General Wool to Norfolk. Stanton and Lincoln returned to Fort Monroe. Shortly thereafter, for one of the few times in his presidency, Lincoln lost control and displayed anger. He discovered that General Mansfield's troops were not taking part in the attack on Norfolk. In anger, President Lincoln threw his hat on the floor and dictated an order committing those troops immediately.

Mr. Lincoln retired to bed between 9:00 p.m. and 10:00 p.m. in Quarters No. 1. About an hour later, General Wool arrived and proudly announced the fall of Norfolk. This was a real military prize.

William W. Lamb, the mayor of Norfolk, had met General Wool and dragged out the surrender ceremonies until a demolition crew could wreck the Confederate Navy Yard. The *Virginia*, anchored offshore, was now a ship without a port. During the night of May 10, its captain, Josiah Tattnall, took the ironclad to Craney Island and gave the order to destroy the pride of the Confederate navy.

Lincoln received the news of the destruction of the ship at 5:00 a.m. The South no longer had a ship capable of stopping Federal gunboats. Lincoln, on board the USS *Baltimore*, passed within sight of Craney Island and the location of the scuttle. He then sailed up the Elizabeth River. The rest of the day and the night was spent in Norfolk. Lincoln telegraphed Henry Halleck, "Norfolk in our possession, *Merrimack* blown up and *Monitor* and other ships going up the James River to Richmond."

Stories abound of the President's visit to Antietam and then to the army at Falmouth in April 1863. However, few sources exist concerning the visit to McDowell's headquarters in 1862.

McDowell had been advised by Secretary Stanton on May 17 to prepare to move overland on Richmond. This was to occur as soon as he was joined by the troops of James Shields. On May 22, Shields's Division reached Falmouth. They looked in poor form and were in need of shoes, uniforms and supplies. They had been chasing Jackson in the Shenandoah. John Gibbon's men thought they looked like a bunch of "ragamuffins."

These troops were present during the visit by President Lincoln and Secretary Stanton. The President reviewed the troops and then received the officers at the Lacey House (Chatham). This was the large mansion directly across the river from Fredericksburg.

Lincoln had hoped that McDowell could move on Richmond at once. However, even as this was being discussed, Thomas J. Jackson was ready to take Front Royal and then move on Winchester in the northern part of the Shenandoah Valley.

Other sources note that on May 23, Lincoln, Stanton, French Minister M. Mercier and Captain Dahlgren met with McDowell at the Lacey House. James W. Hunnicutt, editor of the *Christian Banner*, wrote:

> *President Lincoln and Hon. Edwin M. Stanton, Secretary of War visited Fredericksburg on last Friday, the 23rd instant. They rode in a carriage drawn by four fine iron-gray horses. They crossed the Rappahannock River on the canal boat bridge, and passed up Princess Anne Street to the Farmers Bank, the headquarters of General* [Marsena] *Patrick, where the carriage stopped about five minutes, and then moved off…to visit some camp of soldiers out of town. A large escort accompanied the distinguished visitors. There were no demonstrations of joy, however, from any of the citizens.*[11]

One of the units at Falmouth, Virginia, in 1862 was the Second Wisconsin. George Otis, the regimental historian, noted that Falmouth "was a thriving little village, at the foot of the falls, where there is great waterpower, nearly opposite Fredericksburg." The lads from Wisconsin enjoyed Falmouth. They bought out three of the stores, using Confederate script. A five-dollar U.S. Treasury note "would buy a basket full of goods, while it required a bushel basket full of Confederate notes to purchase a pound of tea or coffee."[12]

On May 23, the Second Wisconsin was among the units reviewed by President Lincoln. The brigade was complimented for its "splendid appearance.…We look upon the presence of Abraham Lincoln as the forerunner of something to happen."[13]

George Otis of the Second Wisconsin observed, "Our corps is today reviewed by General Joe Hooker, President Lincoln, and Secretary Seward. General Stoneman, of cavalry fame, is also of the party, as is General Sickles, accompanied by his wife, and several other ladies. This review is said to be a fine affair, and for the one hundredth time, more or less, we are flattered with the remark that we are a fine body of brave and gallant soldiers."[14]

John Gibbon was born in Pennsylvania in 1827 but appointed to the United States Military Academy from North Carolina. He graduated in 1847 and served in the Seminole War and later on the frontier. Then Gibbon returned to West Point as an artillery instructor. His family endured the division of the Civil War. Gibbon had three brothers serving in the Confederate army.

Early in the war, Gibbon served as McDowell's chief of artillery. Later, he led the famed Iron Brigade in the First Corps. Gibbon was seriously wounded at Fredericksburg. He was on the disabled list until March 1863 and received a division command in the Second Corps just about the time of Lincoln's 1863 visit.

However, in 1862, Gibbon was among those invited to the Lacey House to meet Mr. Lincoln. Reaching the Lacey House, the officers entered a large hall. Then, according to rank, General McDowell presented his generals to the President. Gibbon wrote:

> We all advanced and shook hands with Mr. Lincoln. The last name seemed to catch his attention and assuming a peculiarly quizzical expression he inquired—"Is this the man who wrote the DECLINE AND FALL OF THE ROMAN EMPIRE?"
>
> Doubtless I looked somewhat confused at this pointed allusion, for placing his hand kindly on my shoulder, he said, "Never mind General, if you will write the decline and fall of this rebellion, I will let you off."

"Why," I said, "Mr. President, the only book I ever did write—the ARTILLERIST'S MANUAL—the War Department refused to subscribe to." He laughingly replied, "I shall have to tell Stanton to give you another hearing."[15]

WEST POINT

The *New York Times*, in its June 26, 1862 edition, noted that "the President is given to unannounced journeying." The writer noted that the recent visits to Fort Monroe and Norfolk were unexpected yet significant and that the last excursion (West Point) was "quite as surprising, taking the whole North by storm." It was almost as though the writer was saying that the President was not expected to travel.[16]

On June 20, the President directed Colonel D.C. McCallum, "formerly of the Erie Railway, but now Military Director of Railways in the United States to prepare a special train to go to New York." The President wanted the trip to be made in utmost secrecy, "unbored and unobserved and to go with speed." The train was prepared and a telegram sent to the superintendent of the Hudson River Road to meet the train from Washington.

On June 23, General John Pope escorted Mr. Lincoln to the Washington Station, and "the express" pulled out at 4:00 p.m. There was no Secret Service or any escort—just Colonel McCallum and, according to the *Times*, Mr. Lincoln's body servant, William.[17]

Mr. Samuel Sloan, president of the Hudson River Road, was at West Point for his summer vacation. Mr. Sloan received a telegram, "PREPARE TO RECEIVE A BROTHER PRESIDENT."

Mr. Sloan was perplexed. He did not know what to make of the communiqué. Aware of the presence of General Winfield Scott at West Point, Sloan contacted the general in Garrison. He stated that he believed that President Lincoln was coming, but why? Had there been a national calamity? Was General McClellan dead? Had there been a major military defeat?

Although still a huge man, General Scott was in better health since he did not have all the worries and responsibilities of the war plaguing his mind and abilities. Together, Sloan and Scott rode down to the ferry at Garrison.

Lincoln respected the veteran General Scott, who was "a year older than the Constitution, and a hero of the Mexican War." Scott had been in

John Gibbon. *Library of Congress*.

command of the Union armies since 1841. When the Civil War began, he was considered too old, too ill and too heavy to retain command. Scott was succeeded by George B. McClellan in October 1861. Scott, a Virginian, was the only "non West Pointer" of southern origin in the Regular Army to remain loyal to the Union.

Scott and Sloan waited and waited. The general sat wrapped in his military cloak, while Sloan paced and pranced. "Hour after hour sped away,

Chatham, visited by both Washington and Lincoln. *Author's collection.*

but still no sign of the President." Curious onlookers had gathered, but as the hour grew later, they departed.

At 1:30 a.m. on June 24, Lincoln changed trains in New York. At last, at about 3:00 a.m., the train whistle was heard on the banks of the Hudson at Garrison. Sloan and McCallum escorted the President to General Scott, waiting on the ferryboat.

"My dear General, I'm glad to see you, there's nothing wrong I assure you," said Mr. Lincoln as he warmly grasped the hand of the aged military leader. The group then went to the Crozzen's Hotel in West Point. The journey on land was made through the rain and mud.

The twenty-fourth was a busy day. Mr. Lincoln entered the dining hall alone. Mr. Sloan spoke briefly to him. Then the President and General Scott retired to a private parlor, where there were maps and charts. The doors were locked, and a waiter stood guard to prevent any intrusion. The two conferred until noon. Mr. Lincoln consulted Scott, whom he admired and trusted on the conduct of the war. He sought means and methods to bring to the conflict to a speedy conclusion. They discussed troop dispositions.

From noon until 3:00 p.m., Mr. Lincoln toured West Point. Then there was a dinner party at the hotel, and Lincoln toured the Parrot Cold Springs Foundry three miles away. He noted the large shells and the levees. He laughed at a story about a shark that swallowed a red-hot harpoon.

From 9:00 p.m. to 11:00 p.m., Lincoln received guests in the hotel parlor. A writer from the *Utica Gazette* was unhappy that "the irrepressible of the New York papers found their way to West Point during the President's late flying visit."[18]

Encampment at West Point. *Library of Congress.*

Somehow, there must have been a security leak, as a group gathered on the portico of the hotel to serenade the President. Lincoln was exhausted and did not hear the music. He was "sound asleep and unwakable by any noise save, possibly the fall of Richmond." The writer noted, though, "It is a pity that the President did not hear the serenade, for the selection of music was good and the execution perfect."

Scott and Lincoln spent a little more time together on June 25. Then at 10:10 a.m. the President, General Scott, Mr. McCallum and the reporters left West Point.

Speculation was rampant. Some felt that there would be a cabinet shakeup. Others thought there might be major change in military strategy. Still others thought that perhaps General Scott might take command of the Union armies. Both General Scott and the President were smiling and upbeat.

The train left with full steam ahead. Folks were amazed that the Hudson Line made the trip from Tarrytown to New York City in twenty-five minutes. The news had preceded the train. All along the line, there were citizens gathered to "see the head of the Nation." When the train slowed or stopped, he was given bouquets of flowers. Young and old cheered and shouted. "In a word, he looked and felt happy." He and the people seemed to be one.

General Scott was very much impressed with the lean, lank man from Illinois. He believed the President to "be a man of clear head, good heart, and strong will." Scott was also impressed with Mr. Lincoln's "grasp of military necessities."

Mr. Sloan had telegraphed his New York offices, directing that all the employees to be at the depot when the train rolled in. Thus, lusty cheers filled the air as the train slowed to a halt. However, the stop was very brief, and the President did not have the opportunity to give a speech the crowd requested.[19]

Then it was on to Jersey City. At 11:00 a.m., Inspector Leonard and two patrolmen had gone to the depot for crowd control. About one hundred were on hand as the President arrived via ferryboat and carriage to the Jersey City terminal. The train was short, an engine and "two handsome new cars." As the President and Colonel McCallum stepped from the carriage, they were completely surrounded. New York police helped to clear a passage. They were assisted by J.W. Woodruff, assistant superintendent of the New Jersey Railroad.[20]

President Lincoln then boarded the train. He stood on the platform of the rear car. The crowd applauded and called for a speech. Mr. Lincoln removed his hat, and they cheered even more. Then he told the crowd that his visit with General Scott at West Point was not as important as many thought. "I can only remark that it had nothing whatever to do with making or unmaking any General in the country." At this, the crowd laughed and clapped. "The Secretary of War, you know, holds a pretty tight rein on the Press, so that they do not tell more than they ought to: and I am afraid that if I blab too much, he might draw a tight rein on me." At that, roars of laughter and more applause filled the air.

Harrison's Landing

By July 7, Mr. Lincoln was traveling again. The Peninsula Campaign was over. The flag of the Confederacy still fluttered over Richmond. And there was disenchantment with George B. McClellan, the "Little Napoleon." He talked a better campaign than he fought. McClellan was always in need: more men, more horses and more supplies. Lincoln was unhappy. Thus, the President and his party departed Washington at "an early hour aboard the USS *Ariel*." Destination: Harrison's Landing. McClellan had moved the Army of the Potomac to the landing on July 3. Here the command would remain until mid-August.

During the Civil War years, Berkeley Plantation and Harrison's Landing were synonymous. Berkeley was the birthplace of President William Henry Harrison. And during the Peninsula Campaign, it was McClellan's headquarters. It also served as an army hospital and signal station. It was here that General Daniel Butterfield conceived the bugle call that we now know as taps.

The *Ariel* docked early in the morning. Lincoln conferred with Ambrose Burnside shipside. Later, General Dix and his staff called on the President. The President had landed at Fort Monroe. Thus, it wasn't until midmorning that the *Ariel* steamed up the James River to Harrison's Landing. The Presidential party arrived at 6:00 p.m. Cannons from Flag Officer Goldsborough's ship fired salutes. Mr. Lincoln reviewed the troops until darkness fell. He rode by waving his stovepipe hat.[21]

After Lincoln returned to the *Ariel*, General McClellan came aboard. Never short on advice, the general presented Mr. Lincoln with his "Harrison Landing's Letter." This contained his views and beliefs on the future conduct of the war. The President read the letter at once but made no comment on the contents. The letter was not published until after

A James River plantation,

Berkeley Plantation. *Berkeley Plantation*.

McClellan was relieved from command in November. However, the material in the letter did not help him. It helped to consolidate the disdain and hostility with which he was held.

On July 9, Lincoln conferred with many officers in the Army of the Potomac on military matters. He recorded the comments.

Visits to campsites followed, and there were some reviews. Mr. Lincoln expressed satisfaction at the condition of the troops. He declared, "I wanted to see for myself." Rumor had it that the Presidential visit was a prelude to another "On to Richmond" move.

July 10 brought the departure from Harrison's Landing. The *Ariel* stopped briefly at Fort Monroe. Lincoln visited some of the artillery batteries and received a salute. He dined with General Burnside aboard the *Alice Price*. The Presidential party left Fort Monroe at 4:30 p.m. Mrs. Lincoln was also traveling at the time—she was in New York on a shopping trip.[22]

Trouble seemed to plague Lincoln. The ship ran aground on Kettle Shoals, and several hours were spent getting the ship to float. The delay apparently allowed Lincoln and his companions to go swimming. Colonels Blair and James Nagle accompanied the President on his return trip.

Lincoln had demonstrated anger during his visit to the army in May. However, with George B. McClellan, he was most patient. Whether he believed in McClellan's potential or whether he had no other choice, it is difficult to tell.[23]

Lincoln's woes continued in the summer of 1862. After the failure of the Peninsula Campaign, the Army of the Potomac was withdrawn to Aquia Creek. The War Department took John Frémont's Mountain Department, Nathaniel Banks's Department of the Shenandoah and Irvin McDowell's Department of the Rappahannock. These commands were formed into the Army of Virginia and placed under the command of John P. Pope, who alienated his new command by giving an address after assuming command that seemed to cast a negative light on the previous actions of the troops. He angered Robert E. Lee by prescribing harsh treatment of the South.

Furthermore, Pope bragged that where he came from, they were used to seeing the backs of the enemy. He also stated that his headquarters would be in the saddle.

John Pope did not last long. The armies of Virginia and Potomac did not cooperate very well, and Pope had never faced the likes of Thomas J. Jackson and Robert E. Lee. Jackson launched a wide flanking march. In late August, the Army of Northern Virginia massed on the fields of First Manassas to inflict yet another defeat on Union arms. The men in blue fell back on the defenses of Washington in disarray. John Pope was gone, and George B. McClellan was called on to save the Union cause.

Flushed with victory and hoping to add Maryland to the Confederacy—and perhaps gain recognition from France and England—Lee, in early September, put his columns in motion. The Army of Northern Virginia crossed the Potomac at White's Ford and moved on Frederick, Maryland. There it camped and awaited developments.[24]

Lee thought that the Union garrison of twelve thousand, located at Harpers Ferry, twenty miles southwest of Frederick, would be withdrawn. When it was not, he devised Order No. 191 and divided his army into five segments to capture Harpers Ferry. As long as a large detachment of Union troops was located there, they would be a threat to his rear, supplies and communications. The Union Army of Northern Virginia marched from Frederick on September 10 to fulfill its mission.

Meanwhile, McClellan moved leisurely northward on three roads. He covered the thirty-five miles from Rockville to Frederick in one week. On Saturday, September 13, he received a great welcome in Frederick. Additionally, some of his men found a piece of paper, a lost copy of Order No. 191. He had a golden opportunity to thrust between the divided elements of Lee's army and defeat them in detail. However, speed was not one of McClellan's notable traits.

On Sunday, September 14, Union troops tramped through the streets of Frederick, headed for the South Mountain passes. At various times during the day, heavy fighting occurred at Crampton's, Fox's and Turner's Gaps. Basically, the Confederate rear guard remained firm. However, the Middletown Valley was full of white covered wagons and long lines of men in blue. Lee said, "The day has gone against us. We will regroup at Sharpsburg."[25]

As Monday, September 15 dawned, about half of Lee's army began filing into position on the ridges north and south of the village of Sharpsburg. Lee had but eighteen thousand men present for duty. Another seventeen thousand under the commands of Jackson and McLaws had surrounded

Harpers Ferry from Bolivar Heights, Maryland, and Loudoun Heights in Virginia. A little after 8:00 a.m., the Union garrison surrendered, the largest capitulation of American forces until the fall of Bataan and Corregidor in the spring of 1942. Jackson dashed a note to Lee at Sharpsburg and made plans to immediately move his command northward.

Lee had the Potomac River four miles in his rear, and he confronted an enemy that was just several hours' march away. He could have been overwhelmed. Once again, McClellan moved too slowly. Several years after the campaign, many experts felt that McClellan had fought the Battle of Antietam or Sharpsburg one if not two days too late.

September 16 was a day of the gathering of the hordes. Smoke from the "fires of a hundred circling camps" filled the Antietam Valley. It was the eve of the seventy-fifth signing of the Constitution. The battle might decide whether or not there was still a nation. As darkness fell, soldiers wrote notes to loved ones and pinned the addresses of the next of kin to their clothing just in case they "would be numbered among the fallen."

With the dawn of September 17, the cannons began to boom. The Union infantry moved forward, heading south to Confederate positions about half a mile away. From sunrise to sunset, the battle raged between the village of Sharpsburg and the Antietam Creek. McClellan committed his commands one by one. The battles raged in the bloody cornfield of D.R. Miller, a Dunker and a pacifist. Then the carnage shifted to the West Woods, and the tide of battle surged around the little white brick Dunker Church. By midmorning, the sounds of battle had shifted to a sunken country road connecting the Hagerstown Pike with the Boonsboro Pike. For three hours, two divisions of the Union Second Corps attacked Confederate defenders in the Sunken Road. Still later, the Union Ninth Corps carried the Lower Bridge and, after a two-hour delay, began sweeping forward to Sharpsburg. However, A.P. Hill had left Harpers Ferry early in the morning with several thousand men. The command marched seventeen miles, forded the Potomac River and then launched a counterattack into the Union flank, turning back the threat to the Confederate rear. Hill had saved the day.

At last, the sun went down in the west. The fighting had raged in the Miller Cornfield, in the West Woods, around the Dunker Church, near the Sunken Road and at the Stone Bridge. Brave men met brave men. "The Landscape Turned Red." It was America's bloodiest day, even worse than many of the future battles of World War II—12,400 Union soldiers were dead, wounded or missing. In the ranks of the Army of Northern Virginia, 10,700 were among the fallen. This was almost 1 of every 3 men present for duty. About 5,000 were dead or would die; 18,000 were nursing wounds. The Hagerstown paper noted, "The area is one vast hospital."[26]

The two armies remained on the field during September 18. When night came, Lee and the Army of the Potomac crossed the Potomac at Shepherdstown Ford. The Maryland Campaign was over. Although technically the engagement was a draw, politically and economically it was a Union victory. In those days, the army that left the field first was considered the vanquished. When England and France received the news that the South had not been victorious north of the Potomac, they placed diplomatic recognition on hold. But there was even more significance to the battle that had raged on the banks of Antietam Creek.

When the news of Antietam reached the White House, Mr. Lincoln put on his glasses and opened a desk drawer. He pulled out some papers and put the finishing touches on an important document, calling a cabinet meeting for Monday, September 22.

Monday morning came and with it one of the great moments in American history. After reading a funny chapter from Artemus Ward's *High-Handed Outrage at Utica*, the President became very solemn:

Gentlemen, I have, as you are aware, thought a great deal about the relation of this war to slavery; and you all remember that several weeks ago, I read to you an order I had prepared on the subject, which on account of the objects made by some of you, was not issued. Ever since then, my mind has been much occupied with this subject, and I have thought all along that the time for acting on it might very probably come. I think the time has come now. I wish that we were in a better condition. The action of the army against the rebels has not been quite what I should have best liked. But they have been driven out of Maryland, and Pennsylvania is no longer in danger of invasion. When the rebel army was at Frederick, I determined, as soon as it should be driven out of Maryland, to issue a Proclamation of Emancipation such as I thought most likely to be useful. I said nothing to any one; but I made a promise to myself, and [hesitating a little]—to my Maker. The rebel army is now driven out, and I am going to fulfill that promise. I have got you together to hear what I have written down. I do not wish your advice about the main matter—for that I have determined for myself. This I say without anything but respect for any one of you. But I already know the views of each on this question. They have been heretofore expressed, and I have considered them as thoroughly and carefully as I can. What I have written is that which my reflections have determined me to say. If there is anything in the expressions I use, or any other minor matter, which any one of you thinks had best be changed, I shall be glad to receive the suggestions. One other observation I will make. I know very well that many others might, in this matter, as in others, do better than I can; and if I were satisfied that the public confidence was more fully possessed by any one of them than by me, and knew of any Constitution way in which he could be put in my place, he should have it. I would gladly yield it to him. But though I believe that I have not so much of the confidence of the people as I had some time since, I do not know that, all things considered, any other person has more; and however this may be, there is no way in which I can have any other man put where I am. I must do the best I can, and bear the responsibility of taking the course of action which I feel I ought to take.[27]

President Lincoln then read a document that would become one of the milestones of America. The document had cost the President "blood, sweat, and tears." He felt he had to do it. He promised God that he would do it if given any sign of a military victory, and about a week before Antietam, he made his final decision. Who are we to say that the Emancipation Proclamation was not the righteous sentence of God, given to the world through His servant Abraham Lincoln? Lincoln read:

That, on the first day of January, in the year of our Lord one thousand eight hundred and sixty-three, all persons held as slaves within any State or designated part of a State, the people whereof shall then be in rebellion against the United States, shall be then, thenceforward, and forever FREE; and the Executive Government of the United States, including the military and naval authority thereof, will recognize the freedom of such persons, and will do no act or acts to repress such persons, or any of them in any efforts they may make in their actual freedom.[28]

Secretary Seward interrupted the President, saying, "I think, Mr. President, that you should insert after the word 'recognize,' in that sentence, the words 'and maintain.'" Lincoln replied that he had already thought of the words but was not sure he could support them if inserted. Seward insisted, however, and the words were inserted.

On Monday morning, September 24, the preliminary Emancipation Proclamation was published for all the world to see. It seemed for some like God's "Righteous Sentence."

The President's act had been like a chemist tossing a tiny pinch of a powerful ingredient into a seething and shaking cauldron. Colors and currents shifted and deepened. New channels cut their way to the surface. Below the fresh confusion was heaving some deep and irrevocable change.

A new thought was found in the words of the President's proclamation. An old way of life was dying. Perhaps it would take a long time to see the ultimate truth of the message, but something was being born in the midst of a terrible war.

Toward the end of September 1862, Mr. Lincoln wrote a riddle. He had given much thought to the question. The riddle was left on his desk—not for publication. John Hay made a copy of it. The President had written:

> *The will of God prevails. In great contests each party claims to act in accordance with the will of God. Both may be, and one must be, wrong. God cannot be for and against the same thing at the same time. In the present civil war it is quite possible that God's purpose is something different from the purpose of either party; and yet the human instrumentalities, working just as they do, are the best adaptation to affect his purpose. I am almost ready to say that this is probably true; that God wills this contest, and wills that it shall not end yet. By his mere great power on the minds of the new contestants, he could have either saved or destroyed the Union without a human contest. Yet the contest began. And having begun, he could not give the final victory to either side any day. Yet the contest proceeds.*[29]

One of the greatest consequences of the American Civil War was the Emancipation Proclamation. After Antietam, the country was set on a new course, a course from which there could be no turning back. "Here at last was the sounding forth of the bugle that would never call retreat."

HARPERS FERRY AND ANTIETAM

At 6:00 a.m. on Wednesday, October 1, a train departed from Washington, D.C. It headed northeast to Relay and then west to Frederick and Point of Rocks. At noon, the train finally reached a point across the Potomac River from Harpers Ferry, Virginia (West Virginia had not yet become a state).

On board were John W. Garrett, the president of the Baltimore and Ohio Railroad; John McClernand, a democratic political general from

Illinois; Ozias Hatch, a government leader from Illinois; Joseph Kennedy, superintendent of the census, an agency similar to the current Department of Commerce; Ward Hill Lamon; and none other than the sixteenth president of the United States, Abraham Lincoln.

Mr. Garrett had apparently suggested the trip. The B&O Railroad was instrumental to the Union war effort, ferrying supplies. Lincoln appreciated Garrett's loyalty and felt that he owed him a debt of gratitude. Besides, the journey would get Lincoln out of Washington. He could confer with George B. McClellan, attempting to get the Army of the Potomac moving after Lee, and Mr. Lincoln could visit the troops, thanking them in person for their gallantry at Antietam.[30]

Harpers Ferry did not present a very pretty picture. Although the scenery was as lovely as ever, the town had been ravaged by both armies. The Confederates had seized the U.S. Arsenal, or the remains of it, in April 1861. Realizing the strategic importance of Harpers Ferry, it was occupied by the Confederates until the middle of June 1861. It was here that Thomas J. Jackson had trained and formed five Virginia regiments into a unit later to

Harpers Ferry in 1862. *Library of Congress.*

LINCOLN'S WARTIME TOURS FROM WASHINGTON, D.C.

be known as the Stonewall Brigade. Before the spring of 1862, the Federals moved from Harpers Ferry toward Winchester on February 22, 1862. Jackson was back briefly in May and then occupied Harpers Ferry in mid-September 1862, receiving the surrender of the garrison. A member of the Nineteenth Maine noted that the stately walls of the homes were crumbling, most were windowless and many were charred from fires from the previous winter.

Upon reaching Harpers Ferry, the Presidential party left the train and crossed the Potomac River on a pontoon bridge. The regular bridge had been destroyed by Confederate troops two weeks earlier.

The Union Second Corps had been the first to depart from Antietam and was now camped around Harpers Ferry. Lincoln was met by Edwin Vose Sumner, the commander of the Second Corps. He was taken on a tour of Bolivar Heights and reviewed some of the troops. McClellan rode from his headquarters south to Sharpsburg to meet and confer with the President.

Ever mindful of Mary, Lincoln had his close friend Ward Hill Lamon go to the telegraph office to send a message confirming his safe arrival. Just a few years ago, Robert O'Connor, who has written several historical novels, discovered the telegram:

Oct. 1, 1862

Gen. McClellan and myself are to be photographed by Mr. Gardner if we can be still long enough. I feel Gen. McClellan should have no problem on his end but I may sway in the breeze a bit.[31]

There are but few accounts of October 1. There were cheers and a twenty-one-gun salute when the President arrived. Colonel Bruce of the 20th Massachusetts wrote, "President Lincoln, along with Generals McClellan and Sumner visited our campsite." A writer for the 108th New York noted, "The President was greeted with thunderous applause." Oliver O. Howard, commanding the division formerly led by the wounded John Sedgwick, wrote:

He was received everywhere with satisfaction, and at times with marked enthusiasm, as he reviewed the troops. At Harper's Ferry I saw him and heard him relate a few of his characteristic anecdotes. He noticed a small engine run out from the bridge, through the village of Harper's Ferry, below the bluff, which gave a peculiar shrill and mournful whistle as its shadow fled rapidly around a hill and passed out of sight. Mr. Lincoln inquired what was the name of that little engine. When told the name, alluding to the panic and terror at the time of John Brown's visit to Harper's Ferry, he said that, in honor of the Virginians of that day, it might well have been named "The Skeered Virginian." He admired the horsemanship of Captain Whittlesey, and when someone said, "That officer was lately a parson," he looked pleasantly after him as he galloped off to carry some order, and remarked, as if to himself, "Parson? He looks more like a cavalier." Thus humorously, and with seldom a smile on his sad face, he moved around among us.[32]

The *New York Herald* cost two cents at that time. Its correspondent wrote that "a brilliant cavalcade reviewed Sumner's splendid corps on Bolivar Heights.…The President also visited the ruins of the railroad bridge and the government buildings."[33]

A telegram was sent to army headquarters south of Sharpsburg advising the commander that President Lincoln was coming. Major Granville O. Haller got busy and found three large tents and bedding for the Presidential party.

David Strother ate supper with General William Franklin, commander of the Sixth Corps. He shared with Strother the account of his command and the fighting at Crampton's Gap. When the evening meal was finished, Strother heard the news that the President was spending the night in Harpers Ferry and would "not be here until tomorrow.…His suite are military men and not Congressmen, thank Heaven."

On Thursday morning, October 2, Mr. Lincoln crossed the Shenandoah River and visited soldiers of the Second Corps. Little or nothing exists of that visit. Then it was back to Harpers Ferry and across the Potomac—the commencement of the trip to Antietam.

En route, elements of the Twelfth Corps were visited on Maryland Heights. Charles Morse of the Second Massachusetts said that Lincoln started for the summit, but when he that saw the path was almost straight up, he turned back. Lincoln chatted with A.S. Williams, commander of the Twelfth Corps. The general, despite the demands on his time, always wrote to his daughters in Detroit. In his October letter, he noted:

The President was here a few days since. I had quite a long talk with him, sitting on a pile of logs. He is really the most unaffected, simple-minded, honest, and frank man I have ever met. I wish he had a little more firmness.[34]

Alpheus S. Williams. *Library of Congress*.

Justin Hinkley of the Third Wisconsin wrote:

> *We got to see Mr. Lincoln....He came entirely unannounced, but we hurriedly turned out the Regiment and presented arms.*[35]

Edmund Brown of the Twenty-Seventh Indiana related:

> *While we were on the slopes of Maryland Heights President Lincoln made a visit to the army. No reviews were held, as was the case later, but the President rode around among the camps extensively. He was brought up to the camp of our brigade, though, while the Twenty-Seventh had orders to form in line and be ready to receive him....We were permitted only to see the company of horsemen at a distance.*[36]

The *New York Herald* noted that Lincoln left Harpers Ferry at noon and rode to McClellan's headquarters. Quoting from the paper, "The President is in excellent health and spirits, and is highly pleased with the good condition of the troops. The President manifested greatest interest in everything connected with our recent victory."[37]

After visiting the troops, the President was back on the Harpers Ferry road on the Maryland side of the river. Near the intersection with the Mills Road south of Sharpsburg, he was met by Ambrose Burnside, the bewhiskered commander of the Union Ninth Corps. His command had been involved in the attack on the Lower Bridge and was now camped along the Mills Road.

As Lincoln was arriving sometime in the afternoon, the Union First Corps was drawn up in the fields just north of the current Sharpsburg Elementary School, waiting to be reviewed by the President. However, it was a classic army "hurry up and wait." The men formed and waited. Then came the word that the President would be late. The review was postponed until the next day. Needless to say, there were a lot of unhappy soldiers.

For many years, there was a question as to the location of McClellan's headquarters and the site of Lincoln's quarters during his Antietam visit. It was known that McClellan had moved his headquarters from the Pry farm on September 20 to a point three miles south of Sharpsburg. But where? The answer remained hidden for almost 140 years. Then the eminent historian Dennis Frye and his wife bought the historic farm where Burnside maintained his headquarters after Antietam. This was the Raleigh Showman property on the north side of Mills Road. While doing research on his property, Dennis found a War Damage Claim filed by Keziah and Otho Showman for damages incurred while their property was being used as headquarters for General McClellan and during the visit of President Lincoln. The Otho Showman property was east of Burnside's headquarters on the south side of the Mills Road. Thus at last the site was discovered.

A large tent was erected for the President and his party. However, whether it was on the north or the south side of the road is not known. Nearby were the camps of Ninth Corps. Edwin Lord of the Ninth New Hampshire gave us a graphic description:

> *As far as the eye could see reach the fields were dotted over with white tents…..Nearby…were the baggage and supply wagons of the…surrounded by a circle of noisy hungry mules….In the neighboring woods were the numerous camps of cavalry….Campfires burned brightly and each tent displayed candles.*[38]

Although the Otho Showman family presented the damage claim, a Lieutenant Chandler noted that Lincoln spent one night at McClellan's headquarters and the second night stay at Burnside's headquarters.

Once again, Lincoln and McClellan met to talk strategy and the conduct of the war. Two bands serenaded the President, and he wrote a few letters. It was a typical, cool night. The dawn of Friday, October 3, brought sadness as well as a busy day—the only full day of the visit at Antietam.

As daylight began to break over the campsites along the Mills Road, there was the smell of coffee being prepared and perhaps slabs of bacon being fried. Mr. Lincoln and his friend Ozias Hatch took a walk among the troops in the tented city. Lincoln admired Hatch and confided in him. He was one of the men who orchestrated Lincoln's campaign for the presidency. As they walked and talked, Lincoln inquired, "What do you see Hatch?" Mr. Hatch paused for a moment and replied, "Why I see the Army of the Potomac." To this Lincoln responded, "No Hatch, no. This is McClellan's bodyguard."[39]

After breakfast, it was time for one of McClellan's favorite items: the pomp and circumstance of the military. Thus, the general, the President and everybody mounted up. They took the brief ride west on Mills Road to the Raleigh Showman property, Burnside's headquarters. There in the fields north of the Showman house, where the crops had been harvested, the Ninth Corps was formed for reviews. The cannons fired the twenty-one-gun salute. McClellan riding "Little Dan" looked like the Little Napoleon.

Troops had moved by way of the "Antietam Iron Works to more level ground on the east side of the Antietam, and went into camp near a brick house, making shelter of rails and cornstalks.…Our first grand review of the Ninth Army Corps…was held…in the fields north of our campground, the President, Lincoln himself riding past, accompanied by generals McClellan, Burnside and others—all smiling and apparently on the best of terms with each other."

Dr. Ellis reports that there were a lot of spectators present, and cheers filled the air for both the President and McClellan—but McClellan got the most. Ellis felt that the visit was good because the Emancipation Proclamation had caused a lot of unrest in the regiments from Maryland, West Virginia, Pennsylvania, New York and the West.[40]

But no doubt they felt like David Lane, who was "gratified to see 'a live President' and, above all, 'Old Abe.'" Lane seems to be the only writer to leave the impression that Lincoln looked good at Antietam. Lane felt that he was better looking than his pictures—and not "so long and lank."

Raleigh Showman Farm, site of the Ninth Corps review, October 3, 1862. *Author's collection.*

James Oliver was a young doctor from Athol, Massachusetts, in October 1862. He had been attached to the Twenty-First Massachusetts Infantry. On September 17, Oliver treated the wounded at the Henry Rohrbach farm. From October to December 26, Oliver treated the wounded of the Ninth Corps at the Crystal Spring, also known as the Locust Springs. However, on October 3, his main concern was to see the President of the United States. He wrote in his journal:

Oct. 3, 1862
Antietam, Maryland

At eight o'clock the troops were paraded in a large field for the purpose of being reviewed by the President and Gen.'s McClellan and Burnside, who made their appearance about ten o'clock, with their usual staff.

I looked with eager eyes upon Lincoln—had a fine view of him as he paraded along the lines. Oh! he is homely **beyond all description**. *There may be great executive power there also, but he looks like a very inferior centre piece for this Republic. A responsibility rests upon him which has never in all history been equaled. Most earnestly I hope he will faithfully perform his many duties to his country, and through his wisdom and energy inspire and encourage the army to do the same.*

Lincoln and McClellan at Antietam. *Library of Congress.*

Enough of the President, and I'll pass along to Burnside who rode next to the President pointing out the troops under his command. There is not a nobler looking man in the service than he is; hope he is as good as he looks.

Just behind Lincoln rode McClellan a regular fop. I feel sick at heart at times to see the Republic, once the pride of all nations, fading out slowly but surely, in the hands of such brainless, heartless, deceiving—men.

Every man in whom any power of a nation like the U.S. (or any other nation) is vested, should be a whole-souled upright man, but I fear there are but few such men at the head of our government. That man in whom the North has placed such implicit trust is no General, no man, but is selfish, vain, and I am tempted to say, soulless.[41]

Edward Lord of the Ninth New Hampshire related:

October 3 was a red-letter day in camp, for the army was reviewed by President Lincoln and General McClellan....The review was announced at rollcall, and immediately all set to work to make themselves look as well as possible. About eight o'clock the regiment was marched to a field designated for the review of the division and formed in line. The division consisted of sixteen regiments of infantry, one of cavalry, and two six-gun batteries, and made a fine appearance.

The regiments were drawn out in one continuous line, with intervals of few rods between the battalions, and with their polished muskets gleaming in the bright sunlight, and their colors—some of them bullet-ridden and blood stained—floating softly in the gentle breeze, awaiting the approach of the reviewing party.

As the President drew near, the artillery thundered a salute, the bands played their loudest and sweetest strains, and from thousands of throats rose cheer on cheer for the great and true-hearted man. "Present arms!" came the command from the officers and up shot the bright bayonets with a simultaneous flash. Again the command, "Shoulder arms!" and like an electric shock down came the burnished weapons. Then came the passing in review.

President Lincoln, mounted on a dark chestnut horse with plain trappings came first, and just behind him was General Burnside. Then came a cavalcade of about fifty civilians, and military officers, and these were followed by the general's bodyguard. The President carried his hat in his hand, and as the party dashed along, first in front and then in the rear of the several brigades, they presented a brilliant spectacle, while the bands played "Hail to the Chief!" with all their might.[42]

Another member of the Ninth New Hampshire noted that there were about twenty brigadier generals in the reviewing party and about ten thousand infantry, in addition to the cavalry and artillery. "Father Abraham passed close by us and looks careworn and thin....General McC looks fat and hearty."

Fitz John Porter's Fifth Corps was camped from the Grove Farm at Mount Airy on the Shepherdstown Road to Antietam Furnace, guarding against

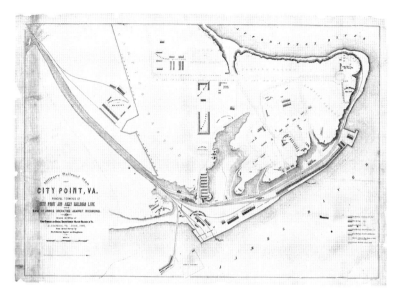

City Point, 1865. *National Park Service.*

any attempts by the Confederates to cross the Potomac. After reviewing the Ninth Corps, Lincoln also had the opportunity to see some of the Fifth Corps troops camped in the area.

The Twentieth Maine did not see action at Sharpsburg. Along with other members of the Fifth Corps, it was in reserve at the Middle Bridge and merely spectated the action. After the battle, the Twentieth was sent to the Antietam Iron Works, where for several weeks the men camped and drilled. A young officer, a former professor at Bowdoin College, studied military strategy and the art of war by the "dim and flaring lamp" in his tent. This was Joshua Chamberlain, the man who was to save Little Round Top—a soldier who was to be designated to receive the surrender at Appomattox.

Like many soldiers, the men from Maine grumbled when they were told they had to march for a review. But the Twentieth Maine never forgot the appearance of Mr. Lincoln. He looked awkward in the saddle. But there was something in his eyes and on his face that inspired courage and loyalty:

> *There were deep lines in his bearded face, there were shadows around the President's eyes. He looked as though he was carrying the burdens of the entire country. McClellan was dressed in his finest, but the soldiers from Maine were more impressed with Lincoln. The tall, humble man from the backwoods of Kentucky was like America at this period in history, a giant emerging from the wilderness. At Antietam, as Lincoln paused and admired*

Chamberlain's white horse, a mystical bond developed between the men from Maine and the man from Springfield. He was one of them.

Chamberlain, one of the war's most decorated soldiers and later president of Bowdoin and governor of Maine, wrote:

We could see the deep sadness in his face, and feel the burden on his heart, thinking of his great commission to save this people, and knowing that he could do this no otherwise than he had been doing…and by and through the manliness of these men—the valor, the steadfastness, the loyalty, the devotion, the sufferings, and a thousand deaths, of those into whose eyes his were looking. How he shrunk from these costly sacrifices, we could see: and we took him into our hearts with answering sympathy, and gave him our pity in return.[43]

A historian of the Fifth Corps simply noted, "Mr. Lincoln came and stayed several days, passing through the different encampments, reviewing the troops, and seeing the battlefields of South Mountain and Antietam."

Dr. Ellis said that the vast amount of men and material stretched for thirteen miles along the Potomac—"the eye never loses sight of the camps."

Dunker Church. *Author's collection.*

Stephen Philip Grove and his wife, Maria, lived at Mount Airy west of Sharpsburg in 1862. President Lincoln spoke with both Mr. Grove and Louisa, age seven, on October 3, 1862.

Louisa Grove was seven years old in 1862. When war came to the Antietam Valley, her parents sent her to stay with friends in Shepherdstown. She had returned and was on hand when the President came to Mount Airy. She never forgot the tall, kindly man who placed his great hand of compassion on her head. With his hand on Louisa's head, he spoke to her parents, expressing regret for the damage done to their farm.[44]

Then the President walked down the big hallway. Wounded were stretched out on both sides. A correspondent with the Presidential party described what occurred next:

> The President…remarked to the wounded Confederates that if they had no objections he would be glad to take them by the hand. He said the solemn obligations which we owe to our country and prosperity compel the prosecution of this war, and it followed that many were our enemies through uncontrollable circumstances, and he bore them no malice, and could take them by the hand with sympathy and good feeling.
>
> After a short silence, the Confederates came forward, and each silently but fervently shook the hand of the President. Mr. Lincoln and General McClellan then walked forward by the side of those who were wounded too seriously to be able to arise and bid them good cheer, assuring them that every possible care should be bestowed upon them to ameliorate their condition. It was a moving scene, and there was not a dry eye in the building, either among the Nationals or Confederates. Both the President and the Generals were kind in their remarks and treatment of the rebel sufferers during this remarkable interview.[45]
>
> The visit to Antietam was not very pleasant for Mr. Lincoln. Not only did he see the devastation of war, and the plight of the wounded, but somewhere near Mount Airy, the president asked Ward Hill Lamon to sing a sad, little song. A presidential favorite was "Twenty Years Ago." Then another member of the group requested "Picayune Butler." This was a lilting comic opera type of song.[46]

Newsmen were nearby and of course heard the music. The dispatches they sent to their home offices carried the news "President Lincoln tours the Antietam Battlefield, and laughs in sight of burial parties." Still others reported the President laughing at the plight of the wounded.

Actually, neither the President nor Lamon saw any burial parties. The battle had been fought two weeks earlier, and the dead had been buried. Truthfully, the President was very much depressed by the things he saw at Antietam. Years before, he had cried when Lamon had sung "Twenty Years Ago." "Picayune Butler" was a harmless effort to cheer the President. The occasion occurred as the Presidential party was leaving Mount Airy.

Of all the criticism Lincoln received during the war years, the account coming from the fields of Antietam hurt him as deeply as any. After the return to Washington, Lincoln and Lamon discussed the possibility of issuing a statement denying the story and telling the truth of the matter. Lincoln said:

> There has already been too much said about this falsehood. Let the thing alone. If I have not established character enough to give the lie to this charge, I can only say that I am mistaken in my own estimate of myself. In politics, every man must skin his own skunk. These fellows are welcome to the hide of this one.[47]

A statement was prepared but never released. Once again the man from the prairies showed his stature and exhibited in person the idea of "with malice toward none."

One cannot help but wonder if the sad event at Antietam might have led to the "few brief remarks" at Gettysburg a year later. Maybe Lincoln would not have gone to the Pennsylvania town had it not been for the sad episode at Antietam. Perhaps the experience at Mount Airy led him to "highly resolve" to say something noble in honor of those "who gave their last full measure of devotion."

Three important events in the life of Lincoln involved Maryland. The first was the arrival of his train in Baltimore in the early morning hours as he traveled to Washington for the First Inaugural. Then, in 1864, he stood on the parapets at Fort Stevens and came under fire during Early's advance on the Capitol. The third and longest visit was to the Antietam Valley in 1862. And although he visited the Army of the Potomac on other occasions, this was the only time Mr. Lincoln was photographed on the battlefield.

Hodgenville, Kentucky; Pigeon Creek, Indiana; Springfield, Illinois; Washington, D.C.; Gettysburg, Pennsylvania—to that list of the places so instrumental in the life of Abraham Lincoln and our American heritage, we add Mount Airy, the Grove Homestead. "It Belongs to the Ages."

President Lincoln at Mount Airy. *Library of Congress.*

Charles Wainwright was an artillery officer in the First Corps. He was from the Hudson Valley area of New York. He and his comrades formed for a big event. There was a thrill in the air, as the third of October came. The men learned that they were to be reviewed by President Lincoln. Just after the noon hour, the First Corps formed a few hundred yards to the rear of what had been the Confederate line of battle. Two o'clock was to be the hour. General Reynolds rode with his staff to meet Mr. Lincoln. The appointment was at McClellan's headquarters, three miles below Sharpsburg. Wainwright went along.

About halfway there, they met Mr. Lincoln, riding in an ambulance with some "Western looking politicians." It was a strange sight—Mr. Lincoln's long legs were doubled up almost to his chin. Wainwright had no time for the Republicans and thought Lincoln to be the ugliest and "most…gawky" man he had ever seen. Reynolds and the staff exchanged greetings with the President and then went to greet McClellan. It was the first time Wainwright had been near enough to get a good look at the commander. He was riding "a splendid bay horse."[48]

The center of the hamlet of Bakersville was the handsome brick Lutheran church, erected in 1854. Nearby were a few homes, a one-room school and many farms.

Ward Hill Lamon. *Library of Congress.*

Hillman Hall was a member of the Sixth New York Cavalry. He noted that on September 20, the members of the regiment unsaddled their horses, the first time in ten days. Four companies were sent east of Sharpsburg to camp on the farm of a Mr. Sherman. Hill had time to ride on his own, and he gave us this report on Sharpsburg: "Its buildings have been bored and well ventilated by the shot and shell of recent battle." Hall had little to say about Lincoln's visit, simply stating, "The Army of the Potomac was reviewed by President Lincoln."

After the Battle of Antietam, the Sixth Corps went to Williamsport to protect the river crossing. But on the twenty-third they returned to the valley of the Antietam, making camp at Bakersville, north of Sharpsburg. Here they remained for several weeks. On the third, they formed on a nice plain to be reviewed by President Lincoln. The booming of the cannons announced his coming. McClellan and General Franklin were with him. The President simply passed along the line. He did not require the troops to march in review. "Repeated cheers filled the air. Sumner's, Burnside's, and Porter's corps had already been reviewed."

The historian of the Sixtieth New York also noted us that there was no attempt to hold a formal review. The appearance of Mr. Lincoln was looked on as a visit. The men in the ranks were in no condition to pass by in review.

The *New York Herald* summarized the day:

> *The President, in company with General McClellan, reviewed today the several corps of the Army of the Potomac, beginning with that of General Burnside, near the mouth of the Antietam, and concluding with that of General Franklin, at Bakersville….At the review of each corps the people collected in large numbers, and manifested the greatest enthusiasm in meeting the President and "Little Mac."*
>
> *Ward Hill Lamon saw David Strother and called him to the President's tent. Mr. Lincoln remembered Strother. David related the details of the cavalry advance to Martinsburg.*
>
> *The day had begun with Lincoln and Hatch walking among the tents of the Ninth Corps, then the review of Burnside's command, a meeting with Joshua Lawrence Chamberlain, a visit to Mount Airy, and the possible birth of the Gettysburg Address, the review of the First Corps, and then the Sixth Corps at Bakersville. The President had indeed been very busy.*

Perhaps Mr. Lincoln experienced some of the sights and sounds described by David Lane:

In the evening, when every tent is lighted up, they present a brilliant and beautiful appearance. "Almost every evening the brass bands of the various regiments delighted the troops "with a concord of sweet sounds."[49]

Saturday, October 4

As the dawn broke, President Lincoln, Ward Lamon, Ozias Hatch, John McClernand and John W. Garrett prepared to leave their tent in the valley of the Antietam and start for home. They were beginning their fourth day in October. There are few accounts of the early morning hours. According to the *Boston Journal*, Mr. Lincoln left McClellan's headquarters at 10:00 a.m. and visited the battlefield of South Mountain, arriving in Frederick at about 5:00 p.m.

Some local tradition says that he was pulled through Sharpsburg in a carriage with white horses and that he was distressed about the folks in the valley losing their pigs, poultry, potatoes and fruits to the soldiers.

Fred Peterman was a walking encyclopedia of Civil War stories. His grandparents saw Mr. Lincoln in a carriage pulled by plumed horses this first Saturday morning in October.

After leaving camp, Lincoln journeyed into Sharpsburg and crossed the Middle Bridge. Young Frisby Keplinger offered him a cold drink of water from a spot near the bridge. Then the Presidential party went to the home of Philip Pry, the location of the Army of the Potomac's headquarters during the Battle of Antietam. Mr. Pry's lovely farm had just about been ruined by the thousands of tenting soldiers. Ambulance and wagon parks filled the fields.

Entering the lovely home, erected in 1844, Mr. Lincoln went upstairs to visit Israel B. Richardson, a general from the Second Corps who had fallen so close to victory at the Sunken Road or Bloody Lane. Richardson had less than a month to live. He died in the room from his wounds on November 3.

According to the Pry family, they offered Lincoln breakfast. Several days later, according to family tradition, they received a thank-you note from 1600 Pennsylvania Avenue.

With camps, the wagon park, army headquarters and a hospital located on their farm, the Prys were virtually ruined financially. They submitted War Damage Claims. However, the government was slow to pay. Therefore, the Pry family packed up and decided to move to a homestead near Johnson City, Tennessee. En route, there was an accident. When a wagon upset, a trunk of personal belongings and personal papers snapped open. The family maintains that one of the items that disappeared was the note from President Lincoln to the family.[50]

Then it was time to leave. There had been a question as to the route of Lincoln's return to Frederick. All three passes in South Mountain had been mentioned as possible routes. However, Edward Itnyre found the answer in the October 10, 1862 issue of the *Middletown Valley Register*.[51] The October 10, 1862 issue stated:

> *Last week President Lincoln accompanied by Gen. McClellan, and staff, several other friends paid a visit to the Army of the Potomac, and after spending several days reviewing the troops, and examining the battlefields of Antietam, returned to Washington, via Boonsboro, Middletown, and Frederick, on Saturday last—Gen. McClellan and staff accompanied the party to within two miles of this place* [Middletown] *when they took leave of the President and returned to headquarters. An enthusiastic reception was given the President at Frederick.*
>
> *Following the account there was a note "For a week past, the weather, during the day has been extremely warm, much warmer than usual."*

Apparently Captains L.S. Marther and Derrickson, young officers on McClellan's staff, accompanied the President, along with a cavalry escort.

Patrick Street was lined with people anxious to see and welcome the President of the United States. Just at this time, a smart shower commenced, accompanied by a heavy wind that raised suffocating clouds of dust. But this could not drive away the crowds, who had anxiously waited for his approach. The procession was led by Colonel Allen, the military governor of Frederick, followed by the ambulances containing the Presidential party, accompanied by a detachment of the First Maine Cavalry. The President was enthusiastically received by the multitude, as he rode at last down Patrick Street to Court Street, where the procession turned off and proceeded to the residence of Mrs. Ramsey, on Record Street, where General Hartsuff was being attended since he had been wounded at the Battle of Antietam. The President had expressed a desire to pay his respects to this gallant soldier on his way through the city.

Hartsuff was a graduate of West Point, class of 1843. Like many other Civil War officers, he saw duty on the plains of Texas and in Florida against the Seminoles. He suffered two severe wounds at South Mountain.

There is one account of what took place inside the Ramsey home, related by a little girl. Alice Frazier was eight years old in the fall of 1862. Like her parents, she was a slave. Her mother, Millie, worked for Dr. William Tyler. On this day, Lincoln went to the home of Mrs. Nellie Ramsey, Dr. Tyler's daughter.

Writing in 1934 and looking back on her life, Alice said that the slaves served the President a bite to eat. And Mr. Lincoln called little Alice to him. He asked her age and gave her a paper bill worth five cents. The cook, Caroline Charlton, sent Alice with the money to Bopst's Store to buy five cents' worth of Rapees Snuff. Alice then recalled the President shaking hands with all who were there.[52]

Edward Marvin was a member of the Fifth Connecticut, on detached duty in Frederick. He was present on that historic October day. Marvin related that a large crowd, many of whom were black, gathered at the door of the Ramsey home. They stood and cheered and cheered. Finally, Mr. Lincoln came out to say a few words. He spoke from the doorsteps. Few remembered what he said, but his "appearance brought faith and hope" to the crowd.[53]

Jacob Englebrecht, the man who recorded so much of the life and times of Frederick in the mid-1800s, noted that it was 5:00 p.m. when the President arrived. "He stopped in our City to [see] Gen. Hartstuff who is wounded and now at Mrs. Ramseys. Court Street—The President Staid in town only about half an hour.…I saw him at Mrs. Ramseys."[54]

According to newspapers and eyewitnesses, Mr. Lincoln made two speeches in Frederick. The first occurred when he came out the front door of the Ramsey home. The folks assembled in the street called for a speech, but the President had little to say:

> *In my present position it is hardly proper for me to make speeches. Every word is so closely noted that it will not do to make a foolish one, and I cannot be expected to be prepared to make a sensible one. If I were as I have been most of my life, I might perhaps talk nonsense to you for half an hour, and it wouldn't hurt anyone. As it is, I can only return thanks for the compliments paid our cause. Please accept my sincere thanks for the compliments paid our cause. Please accept my sincere thanks for the compliment to our common country.*

Mr. Lincoln then reentered the ambulance and was driven to the railroad station, closely followed by the rapidly increasing crowd. The party immediately entered the handsomely fitted cars, which had been in readiness to receive them for nearly forty-eight hours. The President was again loudly called for by the throng of citizens and soldiers, and upon making his appearance, another speech was demanded. He good-naturedly responded:

I am surrounded by soldiers, and a little farther off by the citizens of this good city of Frederick. Nevertheless I can only say, as I did five minutes ago, it is not proper for me to make speeches in my present condition. I return thanks to our good soldiers for the services they have rendered, the energy they have shown, the hardships they have endured, and the blood they have shed for this Union of ours; and I also return thanks, not only to the soldiers, but to the good citizens of Frederick, and to the good men, women, and children in this land of ours, for their devotion in the glorious cause, and I say this with no malice in my heart to those who have done otherwise. May our children and children's children for a thousand generations enjoy these benefits conferred upon us by a united country, and have cause yet to rejoice under these glorious institutions, bequeathed to us by Washington and his compeers. Now, my friends, soldiers and citizens, I can only say once more, farewell.[55]

Lincoln then entered the rear of the car, "amid acclamations of the crowd," and the train moved off. As the people cheered, Lincoln emerged again and waved his hat. In fact, he stood on the rear platform of the car and waved until the crowd disappeared from view.

Like those who assembled later at Gettysburg, the residents of Frederick City and County would long remember the brief visit of Mr. Lincoln, his appearance and his words.

Early in September, the Twenty-Fourth Michigan, a new regiment, left Wayne County and the Detroit area for Washington. After spending three weeks in the capital, the men from Michigan boarded cattle cars on September 30 and started for Frederick. They detrained near midnight and made camp in the nearest field. The next day, better campsites were selected. The men settled down to the task of drilling, washing clothing and fishing in the Monocacy River. The bivouac area was between the river and the railroad.

They had a good spot. On October 4, just about one month after leaving Michigan, the soldiers stood near the tracks and greeted the B&O train bearing President Lincoln back to Washington. He was returning from his visit to South Mountain and Antietam. The President stood on the rear platform, looking tired and worn with care. As the train passed, the men of

THE PRESIDENT'S VISIT TO THE ARMY OF THE POTOMAC—ARRIVAL AT THE STATION AT FREDERICK.—SKETCHED BY MR. HAMILTON.

Abraham Lincoln departing Frederick, October 4, 1862. *John R. Hamilton, Civil War artist for* Harper's Weekly, *October 25, 1862.*

the Twenty-Fourth stood up and cheered. They had heard he was coming. And so they had been waiting for some time to catch a glimpse of him. Never did their deep and abiding faith for "Old Abe" diminish.

In mid-October, the Twenty-Fourth Michigan marched across South Mountain and became a part of the famed "Iron Brigade." As a tribute to their valor at Gettysburg and elsewhere, the survivors of the regiment were among those selected as the "Guard of Honor" on the funeral train that carried Lincoln's body to Springfield in 1865.

Orson Curtis wrote one of the best regimental journals of the war, *The History of the Twenty-Fourth Michigan.* Of October 4, he wrote:

> *President Lincoln passed by our camp, from a visit to recent and neighboring battlefields. He stood at the rear of his train, bowing to us as it slowly moved by. His head was uncovered and he looked careworn from weighty matters upon his mind. We gave him some Michigan cheers as the train moved slowly by.*[56]

So the train was heading back to Washington. Mr. Lincoln had a lot to think about. He was impressed by the beauty of Harpers Ferry and the valley of the Antietam. He was saddened by the suffering of the blue and the gray. His heart was gladdened by the support of the troops and the citizens. He was troubled by a procrastinating general and at the prospects of a long, drawn-out war. A turn for the better had been taken at Antietam, but the war was far from over. There would be more battles, more casualties and more suffering, and somewhere he'd tell America what he thought of the terrible conflict. But for now, the train was carrying him to the White House and a Sunday cabinet meeting.[57]

The Presidential train arrived in Washington at 10:00 p.m. on Saturday. After the battles on the peninsula, at Second Bull Run and at Antietam Creek, Lincoln desired a victory before winter set in. Therefore, in early November, George B. McClellan was removed from the command of the Army of the Potomac. The primary reason: he had "the slows." Ambrose Burnside of Rhode Island was named as his successor. Burnside protested his lack of ability. However, initially, he showed promise. Whereas McClellan moved at the rate of six miles per day, Burnside soon had his men moving twenty miles per day.

The Army of the Potomac was in and around Warrenton, Virginia, west of Washington. Half of the Army of Northern Virginia, Longstreet's Corps, was in Culpeper, twenty miles southwest of Warrenton. "Stonewall" Jackson and his corps were still in the Shenandoah Valley. Burnside aimed to get between the divided wings of Lee's army and deal with each in detail and then march on Richmond by way of Fredericksburg, located midway between Washington and Richmond.

His plan was good, and it may have succeeded if a rising river, bad weather and the late arrival of the pontoons had not enabled Lee to hasten to Fredericksburg and establish an impregnable line of defense on the south bank of the Rappahannock River, from Marye's Heights to Hamilton's Crossing.

Burnside knew that the success of his plan depended on speed. He hoped to cross the Rappahannock and move on Richmond before Lee could get in position. Lincoln felt that the plan would work if Burnside moved rapidly. Burnside had most of his infantry in place on the north bank of the Rappahannock by November 20.

Troops, especially 100,000 of them, needed a lot of supplies. Burnside therefore established a new supply base at Belle Plain, ten miles northeast of Fredericksburg. Wagons, supplies and herds of cattle were brought to Belle Plain and then moved forward to the front-line troops. Soon nearly 117,000 Union soldiers faced 72,000 Confederates, separated by the Rappahannock. The river was four hundred feet wide.

Concerned about the stalemate, Lincoln sent Burnside a telegram on November 25. "If I should be in a boat off Aquia Creek at dark tomorrow [Wednesday] evening, could you, without inconvenience meet me and pass an hour or two with me?" Note the tone—it was a request, not an order.

On the twenty-sixth, Lincoln embarked for Belle Plain. He departed in secrecy, as neither General Halleck nor Secretary Stanton was aware of the journey. The next day, Lincoln conferred with General Burnside aboard the USS *Baltimore*.

Strangely, there is no information on this meeting. Apparently, Lincoln proposed a three-pronged assault on Fredericksburg—one column moving from Port Royal and one from the north side of the Pamunkey, while Burnside attempted to cross the Fredericksburg. The military considered this infeasible.

Mr. Lincoln was probably happy to see 1862 depart. He had been under fire from civilians, politicians and the military. Generals discussed a military dictatorship, and few were pleased with the President. Militarily, the Union had suffered one defeat after another, at least in the east. Stonewall Jackson had roamed at will in the Shenandoah. McClellan failed on the peninsula.

Second Bull Run was another Union disaster, and Fredericksburg was worse yet. The lone bright spot was Antietam. Although tactically the struggle was a draw, Lee's retreat enabled Lincoln to state that on January 1, 1863, the slaves in the rebellious states would be freed. This broadened the military and political scope of the war. Perhaps Antietam saved the Lincoln presidency.

Regardless, after Fredericksburg, the armies settled into winter quarters. The Confederates assumed positions on the south bank of the Rappahannock. The Army of the Potomac was north of the river.

On December 20, the Army of the Potomac struck its tents and marched away from the heights across from Fredericksburg. It was headed for winter quarters along the Potomac River, twelve miles away. The site selected for the winter encampment was Belle Plain, located at the confluence of the Potomac Creek and Potomac River. The day was cold and brisk.

Writing on Christmas Day 1862, Rufus Dawes of the Sixth Wisconsin noted, "We are now in camp near the Potomac River, at a placed called Belle Plain. We have a fine view of the broad river and are pleasantly located. We are building substantial winter quarters and hope to be permitted to remain here all winter."[58]

The men of the Twenty-Fourth Michigan christened their bivouac site "Camp Isabella" in honor of Colonel Morrow's wife. She, along with Mrs. Meredith and the wives of the other officers, joined their husbands at Belle Plain.[59]

Morale in the ranks was low. One soldier wrote, "I am sick to death of disaster, and the fools who bring it upon us." The wind was cold, men were unhappy, Lincoln had not found the right general and there were many desertions.

TRAVELS IN 1863

The year 1863 was a big one. Sam Houston, the great Texas patriot, died. Babies were born in the midst of the war years, among them Henry Ford and William Randolph Hearst. New inventions appeared in America, among them an iron scoop fastened to the front of the steam engine and called a cow catcher. And it was the year roller skates appeared. In France, a chemist invented margarine, and the first subway was opened in London.

The fractured Union was still undergoing birth pangs. The Mississippi River was considered by many to be the western frontier. Beyond the river stretched the endless prairies, waiting to be explored and eventually settled. There were mountains to cross, rivers to ford, rails to lay, crops to plant and natural resources to be discovered. Many diseases had not been controlled. Sanitary conditions were poor. Families were large so that at least several offspring could grow to adulthood. Life expectancy in the United States was just twenty-seven years of age.

The Civil War was approaching the conclusion of the second year of struggle. There had been thousands of battlefield deaths. Young men had been maimed for life. Thousands more had died from disease and epidemics. Few were the homes where the angel of death had not stepped into the family circle. In fact, death had invaded the White House in February 1862. Willie Lincoln, the son of President and Mrs. Lincoln, expired. Sadness reigned.

The military situation was not much better. Burnside then endeavored to make a move in January. This resulted in the infamous "Mud March"; after two and a half months, Burnside was gone, and there was another commander at the helm of the Union army. His name was Joseph Hooker, from the state of Massachusetts. He bore a fine title: "Fighting Joe Hooker."

The war was a learning experience for the military as well as the politicians. None had ever been involved in operations on the scale of the war. Therefore, they experienced on-the-job training as they wrestled with strategy, command, logistics and more.

Part of the scheme was Lincoln's search for a commander. Thus situations that arose during the war years necessitated his travels to army headquarters. Mr. Lincoln had chosen Hooker on January 26. However, he must have had some doubts about the man. He knew that "Fighting Joe" had long held aspirations for high command and was not above knifing others in the back to obtain his goals. Lincoln said of Hooker, "He talks badly." Lincoln did not appreciate that part of Hooker's character. He also infuriated Lincoln when he said after Fredericksburg, "The country needs a dictator."

After the meeting with Hooker, Lincoln sent him a letter. The President advised caution, but it was the kind of letter a father might write to a son. Lincoln said, "Beware of rashness, but with energy and sleepless vigilance go forward and give us victories."

Hooker was forty-four years old, a graduate of West Point and a veteran of the Mexican-American War. For a while, he had lived in California as a private citizen. He had a good record as a regimental, division and corps commander. He was one of the few Union generals who was aggressive. The newspaper writers were the ones who named him "Fighting Joe." He had a reputation as a macho man. He was fond of drink, women and gambling. When under the influence of alcohol, he often said things that got him into trouble.

Hooker quickly made some changes in the alignment of the Army of the Potomac, as well as with top-level commanders. Gone were the grand divisions and wing commanders. The dependable John Fulton Reynolds was placed in command of the First Corps. Darius N. Couch was named the leader of the Second Corps. The flamboyant Dan Sickles was selected for the Third Corps. George G. Meade was retained as the leader of the Fifth Corps. John Sedgwick assumed control of the Sixth Corps. Franz Sigel was replaced by O.O. Howard in the Eleventh Corps, and Henry Warner Slocum led the Twelfth Corps.

A system of leaves was instituted. This reduced the problem of desertions. Hooker and the corps commanders kept the troops engaged in "drills, reviews, and inspections." Hooker also designed distinctive badges for the corps and divisions. Thus units could quickly identify one another. This fostered an esprit de corps.

Along with the corps badge, red, white and blue circles on flags designated divisions. Medical facilities treatment also improved. The result of these positive moves greatly enhanced army morale.

On February 22, the cannons of the Army of the Potomac fired salutes in honor of George Washington's birthday. And there were the proverbial regimental snowball battles. March 17 brought celebrations by the Irish troops, horse racing and wheelbarrow races chasing a greased pig.

The army and veterans of the Second Corps were saddened in March when they learned of the death of the veteran Edwin Vose Sumner, the former corps commander.

March ended and April came. Mr. Lincoln prepared to travel. On Saturday, April 4, 1863, Mr. Lincoln along with his wife, son Tad and some friends rode to the Navy Yard and boarded the dispatch boat *Carrie Martin*. This would be the first of three trips in six weeks to Hooker's headquarters. Others in the Presidential party included Attorney General Edward Bates; Secretary Chase; Dr. Anson G. Henry, a friend from Illinois; Captain Medorem Crawford of Oregon; and Noah Brooks. The craft departed at about 3:00 p.m. The *Carrie Martin* was barely underway when an early spring snowstorm struck. The winds churned the waters, and the going was slow and choppy. The situation became so bad that the captain pulled the craft into a cove opposite Indian Head, Maryland. Without a radio or modern communications, no one knew where the President was. It was an extremely serious situation.

During the stormy night, the men sat up and talked about military strategy and politics. Mr. Lincoln was deeply concerned about what was happening at Charleston. The Union navy was preparing an attack on Fort Sumter.

One of the guests on the trip to Falmouth and Hooker's headquarters was Noah Brooks, a journalist very friendly to the Lincoln administration. Brooks was born in Castine, Maine, in 1830 and in 1854 moved to Dixon, Illinois. There he met Lincoln during the campaign of John Frémont in 1856. Brooks then moved to Kansas and on to California. However, his wife died, and in 1862, he came to Washington. He was surprised to see how Lincoln had changed during the presidency. His appearance was altered by the heavy burdens and duties of the office. "His hair is grizzled, his gait more stooping, his countenance sallow, and there is a sunken, deathly look about the large, cavernous eyes.[60]

Brooks became close to both President and Mrs. Lincoln. As a writer for the *Sacramento Daily Union*, he sent 258 dispatches to his newspaper. These are excellent sources on the day-to-day events of the Lincoln presidency. Brooks wrote under the name of "Castine." In 1895, eight years prior to his death, Brooks published *Washington in Lincoln's Time*. It has become a standard source for information about the Lincoln White House. Brooks also had a lot to say about Lincoln's faith and dependence on prayer.

Along with the President, by request, was Anson G. Henry, Mr. Lincoln's doctor and a close political friend. Henry was born in Richfield, New York, and was five years older than Lincoln. His medical training was on the job with another physician. He did some additional academic work in Cincinnati. He moved a lot and finally settled in Springfield, Illinois, in 1833.

Henry was an active Whig and soon became friends with Lincoln. He campaigned ardently for William Henry Harrison and others. Lincoln felt that his efforts deserved some type of political reward. However, none was forthcoming for Dr. Henry. Later, he and Lincoln supported and stumped for Zachary Taylor. On June 24, 1850, Henry was appointed the Indian agent for the Oregon Territory. He and Edward Baker were close friends. For the next several decades, Henry had his eyes on becoming chief of the Bureau of Indian Affairs.

Henry encouraged Lincoln after the Lincoln-Douglas debates. And he worked with those who helped to gain Lincoln's nomination in 1860. Henry traveled to Washington to visit Mr. Lincoln in February 1863. The doctor also was a close friend of Mrs. Lincoln's. He helped defuse some of the wild rumors about her. After the assassination, Henry remained in Washington for six weeks, comforting and assisting Mrs. Lincoln.

Henry sought the position of commissioner of Indian affairs from Andrew Johnson. Failing in his efforts, he decided to return to California. En route, the ship sank, and Dr. Henry drowned in the seas off northern California.

Brooks was happy to be along on Lincoln's wartime travels. After all, "[i]t is not every day that one can get an invitation to accompany the Commander-in-Chief of the Army and Navy of the United States on an excursion to the vastest army now on the face of the earth."[61] Brooks did not have to think twice when he received the invitation.

Apparently, "the thoughtful wife of the President, an able and noble woman, ought to have the credit for organizing the plan of a tour through the army." She thought that a Presidential visit prior to the spring campaign would be most beneficial. Brooks was surprised at the relaxed manner on board the *Carrie Martin* the night of the storm.

April 7 was Easter Sunday. The snow was still falling when the *Martin* sailed into the harbor at Aquia Creek. Brooks noted that it was an important supply depot. There were huge warehouses. Steamers were tied up at the dock. Daily supplies were brought to the depot and then placed on board trains and taken to the troops in the field. "Enormous freight trains are constantly moving toward the Grand Army which is encamped among the rolling hills of Virginia lying between the Rappahannock and Potomac." About 1 million pounds of forage was needed daily to feed the sixty thousand horses and mules in the Army of the Potomac. Brooks continued:

> The railroad is a temporary affair but well-built and in good running order. When our party started for the special train in waiting there was a tremendous cheer from the assembled crowd who gave another parting peal as the rude freight car, decorated with flags, moved off with the President and suite. The day was disagreeable and chilly, though the snowing had ceased, and the face of the country, denuded of trees, hilly, and white with snow, was uninviting and cheerless. All along the road are camps more or less distant from the track, and the inmates appeared to be comfortably housed from the weather by embankments about their log huts covered with canvass shelter tents. We stopped at Falmouth Station, which is the terminus of the railroad, and is five miles below or east of the old town of Falmouth. The station is an important one and, of course, is now doing a big business in the way of receiving and distributing supplies for the Grand Army. Several carriages and an escort of lancers awaited the President and his party, the honors being done by General Hooker's Chief of Staff, Major General [Daniel] Butterfield. We reached headquarters after a long drive over a fearfully muddy road, the "sacred soil" is red and clayey, almost fathomless in depth, and made more moist by the newly fallen snow.[62]

Falmouth was founded in 1727. It was a trading center for the northern neck of Virginia. The Army of the Potomac camped around Falmouth in November and December 1862 and then again in the spring of 1863 prior to Chancellorsville. It was from this base of operations that the Army of the Potomac headed northward on the roads to Gettysburg.

George Bruce of the Twentieth Massachusetts noted that Falmouth was "situated a mile and a quarter above Fredericksburg on the northerly bank of the Rappahannock at the entrance to a ravine which cuts through the Stafford Hills."[63]

Charles Wainwright, an artillery officer from New York, had some interesting notes about Easter Sunday 1863: "The President arrived at headquarters quite unexpectedly. It is said that their arrival created quite a commotion on Hooker's back stairs, hustling off some of his female acquaintances in a most undignified way."[64]

Wainwright knew that the arrival of the President would mean grand reviews. "Hooker has considerable liking for that sort of thing when he can make it pay; and is said to have boasted while at Washington; declaring that he 'had the finest army on this planet.'"[65] Furthermore, Hooker boasted that he could march the army straight to New Orleans. Wainwright had questions: "Whether or not he will prove capable of taking it as far as Richmond remains to be seen."

Noah Brooks described Hooker's headquarters:

> *General Hooker's headquarters are quite as simple and unpretending as those of any of his men, as he abhors houses and prefers tent life, being unwilling, he says, to live in better quarters than his humblest soldier. The headquarters are about three miles from the Rappahannock in a direct line, situated upon a high, rolling ridge, and not very extensive, as the staff is not large or extravagant. The various staff officers and aides have their tents on either side of what forms a street, at the head of which is the wall tent of General Hooker, which at the time of our visit was flanked by a couple of similar tents put up for the President and his party, who were provided with the luxury of a rough board floor, stoves, camp made bedsteads, and real sheets. The quarters were comfortable and the President and Mrs. Lincoln enjoyed the sharp contrast with the White House hugely, while "Tad," the juvenile Lincoln, had made the acquaintance of nearly every tent before the first day was done.[66]*

MONDAY, APRIL 6

The terrain was still wet and sloppy from the earlier snowfall. Therefore, due to the inclement weather, the grand review was postponed. Lincoln mounted a horse and rode from place to place, visiting the sick and disabled soldiers in the Army of the Potomac.

At 10:00 a.m., Mr. Lincoln received the officers of Hooker's army in his tent. Later in the day, the weather cleared, and the President reviewed the cavalry led by George Stoneman. A twenty-one-gun salute was fired. Mr. Lincoln then watched the squadrons of cavalry ride past, "winding like a huge serpent over hill and dales, stretching far away out of sight." Noah Brooks, the newspaper journalist, described the event:

> [The troops rode by] *banners waving, music crashing, and horses prancing, as the vast columns came on and on.....Never before on this continent was there such a sight witnessed....A GREAT number, assembled together, men and horses, and all looking in excellent condition and admirably fit for service.*[67]

Like all reviews prior to a campaign, there was tinge of sadness. Brooks contemplated the fact that the purpose of "this gorgeous and imposing display is only for the purpose of killing as many men as possible." He also realized that many of the gallant troopers riding in the review would "be numbered with the slain before many days shall pass....Nobody seemed to forget that a battle was not far off but all enjoyed the present." Worry and anxiety were deferred until tomorrow.[68]

During the evening hours, an army band serenaded the President. Joe Hooker was anxious for the reviews to begin. He was at his best in military pomp and circumstance. George G. Meade and Noah Brooks felt that Hooker looked upon the reviews as picnics.

Tuesday, April 7

When it was learned that the President was coming to visit the army, there was a great scurry to get everything ready. The bad weather assisted the officers because it gave them a little more time to prepare.

Nowhere was there more excitement than at Third Corps headquarters. Daniel Sickles was a friend of the Lincoln's, and he relished the prospect of the Presidential visit. There were a lot of women, officers' wives, at Sickles camp. They began digging into their trunks for their best clothing. General Hooker apparently placed the entertainment and social part of the visit in the hands of Dan Sickles. He could not have selected a more qualified person.

Sickles suggested to Princes Salm, the wife of one of his officers, that Mrs. Lincoln be treated like a queen, with the women who were present serving as her ladies in waiting. The women had better sense and rejected most of the idea.

Above: Aquia Creek Landing. *Colonel Jerry Meyers.*

Left: Aquia Creek Landing historic marker. *Colonel Jerry Meyers.*

Most of April 7 was spent at Sickles's headquarters. Lincoln met the officers and reviewed the troops. After the military affairs ended, the Third Corps had a large tent prepared for a reception and cold meats. Sickles was concerned about how haggard Lincoln looked. Therefore, he devised a plan. He wanted officers' wives to encircle the President and kiss him. The women, once again, had better sense. However, Princes Salm managed to kiss him fondly on the cheek.[69]

The President took all this with good humor. Naturally, Mrs. Lincoln was not present. But Tad was, and he shared the news of the event with his mother. Supposedly, she went into a rage. She was furious at Dan Sickles for conceiving the idea and at her husband for going along with it. One observer wrote that "Mr. Lincoln had been subjected to an unhappy quarter of an hour." His wife raked him over the coals.[70]

On April 7, Sedgwick was invited to dine with the Presidential party. However, he was having serious problems with his eyes. It may have been something like pink eye, and he declined. "Uncle John had been bothered with the problem for almost a month and found the situation very troublesome."[71]

Sometime during the day, a member of the Eighth New York Cavalry found time to write to the *Rochester Union and Advertiser*:

> *Yesterday was a great day for the cavalry branch of the Potomac Army, no less an occasion than a grand review by President Lincoln....It was held near Falmouth, on an elevated plain, which afforded a fine range for such a display. I do not expect ever again to witness such an exhibition of "war's magnificently stern array" as was there presented....The President made a better appearance on horseback than I expected to see, but looks extremely thin and careworn, as if his strength would scarcely carry him to the end of his term. As he passed by accompanied by his brilliant escort, it struck me that it would perhaps have been far better for the country if, in the present crisis, the Chair had been filled by a man of military genius like Washington or Jackson, one who could have grasped the sword with his right hand, while he kept the scepter in his left; it may be only a soldier's prejudice, but such was my own reflection and I doubt not also, that of others.[72]*

Wednesday, April 8

This was one of the greatest days on the North American continent. For hours the troops of the Army of the Potomac "passed in review" before the commander in chief. Noah Brooks shared with us the majesty of the moment:

> *April 8 was a gala day in camp....There was a grand review of the infantry and artillery of four corps of the Army of the Potomac,*

namely: the Fifth, the Second, the Third, and the Sixth. The day was brightening. [The weather was better.] *After the usual Presidential salute and cavalcade through the lines, the troops were set in regiments and brigades. It was a splendid sight to witness these 60,000 men all in martial array with colors flying, drums beating, and bayonets gleaming in the struggling sunlight.* [73]

They kept coming and coming. It seemed as though the procession would never end. There were units with new colors and the veteran regiments with colors riddled by shot and shell in the previous engagements of the Army of the Potomac. Some of the units carried streamers with the names of the battles in which they had fought. One of the regiments carried a green flag and the "crownless harp of Erin." [74]

Colonel John D. Wilkins of the Third U.S. Infantry wrote to his wife, stating, "It was a magnificent display of troops and occupied nearly the whole day." He noted of Lincoln, "I think he looks haggard and distressed." Wilkins added, "Mrs. Lincoln was riding in a carriage."

Darius N. Couch wrote:

We had a grand review of the army in honor of the President. The Second Corps paraded with Howard's Eleventh Corps....After I had saluted at the head of my corps I rode to the side of the President, who was on horseback....It was a beautiful stirring sight. Mr. Lincoln, sitting there with his hat off, head bent, and seemingly meditating suddenly turned to me and said, "General Couch, what do you suppose will become of all these men when the war is over." [75]

Couch was pleased to think that someone thought the war would someday come to a conclusion.

President Lincoln rode to the right of General Hooker. Other general officers and their staffs followed. Mrs. Lincoln was in a carriage and apparently remained in a corner so no one could get a good look at her. Tad rode along with another little boy, General Stoneman's bugler. A squadron of lancers brought up the rear. The horses tramped through the mud. During the individual corps reviews, the corps and division commanders rode near the President. Charles Morse of the 2nd Massachusetts noted, "It was a magnificent sight." A member of the 108th New York said that the day brought "probably one of the finest and grandest reviews ever seen on this Continent."

There were also some negative thoughts. An unknown member of the Twenty-Sixth New Jersey wrote, "He [Lincoln] has reviewed the army; let him review himself. Let his aims, his plans…his innumerable blunders pass in review before him. Let him review the past two years, [and] the long line of skeleton forms and weeping widows and orphans moving along in solemn silence."[76]

The historian of the 140th New York noted that Lincoln reviewed the entire Fifth Corps and then stopped by the brigade of Patrick O'Rorke, accompanied by General Hooker and a large group of mounted lancers. While there, the 5th New York demonstrated a favorite bayonet drill. Mr. Lincoln was "very much pleased with it."

Lieutenant Farley was impressed with Lincoln's horsemanship. "His tall, bony figure, dressed in black, riding at the head of that brilliant cortege was a striking one, not to be forgotten by those who saw it."

Farley also noted the stark contrast between the new regiments and the veteran units. The new units had full ranks, while the ranks of the veterans were depleted. The new troops were dressed in sparkling uniforms, while the clothing and flags of the veteran units were tattered. Their trials were told "plainly enough by their scanty numbers and their tattered flags."[77]

Thomas Gawley, a member of the Second Corps and the Eighth Ohio Infantry, was also present for the review:

> *A grand review took place on April 8. About sixty thousand men turned out. President Lincoln, accompanied by part of his cabinet was at the colors.…The review took place on a large plateau about a mile and a half east of our camp, and quite close to the river.…I have never before seen the army in such good physical condition. The men are all fat, healthy well uniformed, thoroughly equipped; the horses are prancing, the guns shining; and everything indicates an army in splendid fighting order.[78]*

Gawley went on to say that President Lincoln wore a plain black civilian suit. He looked wan and pale and presented "an outrageously awkward figure on horseback.…His chin seemed almost buried between the knees of his long bony legs." The picture of Lincoln was in contrast to Hooker, who was well uniformed on a handsome mount and looked every inch the leader.[79]

Some of the troops must not have been impressed. Perhaps their problem was the military tradition of "hurry up and wait." They had to have their equipment in good condition and then were marched to a designated spot before "passing in review."

George Bruce of the Twentieth Massachusetts did not even mention the Presidential visit in his journal. And a member of the First Minnesota simply noted, "Old Abe, his wife and little boy made us a visit and we formed in review.…Would like to have you see the whole Army of the Potomac on review." There was a major problem: there was not enough level ground to get the entire army on. The soldiers of the First Minnesota thought the President "looked rather careworn."[80]

John Gibbon, a division commander in the Second Corps, considered that early April 1863 was "wet, stormy, and very muddy." He felt that his troops made a "fine appearance and I do not think I ever saw them march or look better." Earlier in the war, the regiments in the Philadelphia Brigade were designated as California troops. This was at a suggestion by Colonel (later General) Edward Baker, a close personal friend of Lincoln's. As the troops marched by, Lincoln asked Gibbon to point out the Seventy-First Pennsylvania, one of the units that served under Baker.[81]

Eye and health problems continued to plague John Sedgwick, the leader of the Sixth Corps, on the day of the grand review. He was unable to ride out with his advance troops and meet Mr. Lincoln. However, when the cannons fired the salute, Uncle John rode out to meet the President. It was a proud moment for him. The President sat on a beautiful black steed on an elevated spot with his head uncovered, and the soldiers of the Army of the Potomac marched by. Mrs. Lincoln was in a carriage. Martial music filled the air. "The soldiers marched on a parade field—a plateau two miles back from the Rappahannock River and directly opposite Fredericksburg, in full view of the Confederate forces." Sedgwick noted, "The large review went off very handsomely; troops looked and marched well." Sedgwick and the men of the Sixth Corps greatly appreciated the visit of the President. Private John Fisk of the Second Vermont thought that the "President looked very thin and careworn." The Army of the Potomac "hoped to give the tired chief executive a victory; he had waited long enough."

Chaplain David T. Morrill of the Twenty-Sixth New Jersey wrote:

> As our Regiment passed, the President turned to General Sedgwick…and was heard to say after casting his eye over it and gauging its size and appearance, "That's a splendid Regiment! What a front it presents."… Size…adds much to the impression made by a body of soldiers, and I did not see another in the whole corps, that looked so large [as ours].…It was a striking illustration of the majesty of government to see all the vast army,

embracing officers of every grade and intellects of every caliber and degree of culture paying their respects to one who to all appearance was only a citizen of the republic instead of its President and commander in chief of all its armies. As military as all things were I was glad to be reminded that we still had a civil head.[82]

The Fifth Corps, commanded by George Gordon Meade, was also reviewed on April 8; some sources say that this was on the seventh. Regardless, folks forget times and dates after the passing of time. The men of the Twentieth Maine thought that the President looked "careworn," a favorite expression of that day. He seemed somewhat detached; he was placed on a horse that was several sizes too small for him. His legs looked so long, and his toes almost touched the ground. "The President had neglected to strap down his trouser legs, which had drawn up, revealing the white legs of his drawers. As he jogged along on his little horse, with his tall silk hat jammed down over his ears, the sight was ludicrous and yet no one felt the slightest urge to laugh."

The men from Maine had sympathy for the leader of the nation. He had aged since they had seen him at Antietam in October 1862. His eyes and face were full of a "sense of brooding sorrow and tragic awareness of the destiny in which they were all involved." He seemed to sense what was ahead.[83]

During the trip to Falmouth, Mr. Lincoln visited the army hospitals. Noah Brooks noted that Lincoln visited all the Fifth Corps hospitals, "shaking hands with everyone, asking a question or two…and leaving a kind word here and there. It was a touching scene and one to be long remembered."[84]

Just as he did at Antietam, Lincoln moved among the wounded. He showed them that he cared and was touched by their suffering. Some of the lads shed a tear as the President reached forth his hand to grasp theirs. "No wonder, there was a cheer as Mr. Lincoln left the hospitals."

During the time at Falmouth, the adventurous Tad wanted to see some Rebels. Thus some of the Presidential party went down along the Rappahannock, where the pickets were on outpost duty. Mr. Lincoln gazed across the river to the fields where so many young men in blue had died in December. They saw the Stars and Bars of the Confederacy flying over Fredericksburg. Some Confederate pickets were near a fire located in a chimney that had been destroyed in the earlier action. They spotted Mr. Lincoln and the group, waved and yelled something that could not be distinguished. A Confederate officer looked through his field glasses and bowed. The pickets yelled again.

En route to the First Corps camps, the driver was having difficulties with six stubborn mules. He spoke to them in rather strong, profane language. Mr. Lincoln leaned forward and said, "Excuse me, my friend, are you an Episcopalian?"

"No, Mr. President," replied the teamster. "I'm a Methodist."

"Well," said the President, "I thought you must be an Episcopalian, because you swear just like Governor Seward, who is a church warden."[85]

The driver drove on. The mules received no more comment.

THURSDAY, APRIL 9

Today, it was the turn of the First Corps, commanded by John Fulton Reynolds, to be reviewed:

April 9, the day after the grand review on four corps, the First Corps, Major General [John F.] Reynolds, was reviewed by the President. This corps numbers about 17,000 men and is encamped upon a beautiful plain at the mouth of Potomac creek where it puts into the Potomac river. The day was beautiful and bright, and the scene was one of the finest which we met in our brief campaign. The camp is eight miles from Camp Hooker, and the road thither was over one of the roughest Virginia roads which can be anywhere found. But when reached the parade ground was a choice spot, opening to the broad Potomac river on one side and encircled by half-wooded hills on all the others.

The evolutions of the men were excellent, and the whole spectacle was most inspiriting and superb....One moment feature of this corps is its splendid drum music. The regulations allow one band to each brigade, but many regiments furnish their own bands, and, in some cases, the states pay for the extra bands furnished. In the First and Eleventh Corps drums and trumpets or fifes are the only martial music, and it is preferred by the men for marching as being firmer and more accurate. In some of these drum corps I counted eight snare drums and thirty trumpets, and in others there were seventy-five or eighty drums and half that number of fifes or piccolos. One who has not heard such a band can scarcely imagine the glorious and inspiring effect of the roll and beat of so large a number of drums intermingled with the martial blare of the trumpet and the shriek of the ear-piercing fife. Men who are weary with a hard day's march will pick up enough freshness to march many more hours at the striking up of a band of music, even though it be but a drum and fife.[86]

Louis Shattack of the Sixth Wisconsin described the gala event:

This review was quite an affair. About 30,000 infantry and 10 or 12 batteries of artillery were present. The President rode along the lines mounted on a splendid chestnut charger, accompanied by old Joe and staff and an escort of a regiment of lancers. There is little doubt about "Abe's" ability as a statesman, politician, or rail splitter, but concerning his horsemanship as compared with Joe Hooker, Mrs. Lincoln came in an ambulance and her two boys were there on horseback. This must constitute pretty much the entire household of Father Abraham.

We had a splendid day and a good time generally, only somewhat fatiguing. We got pretty hungry, too, with starting out in the morning and not getting in 'til 4 o'clock.[87]

On April 8, Rufus Dawes of the Sixth Wisconsin was visited by General Meredith at his quarters at Belle Plain and invited to accompany the general on a visit to President and Mrs. Lincoln. For some reason, Dawes refused.

The next day, when the First Division of the First Corps, the "Iron Brigade," marched by "there was a universal manifestation of admiration and applause." The men looked proud. There "was a firm military tread… and exact military movement." It was as though "every company and every regiment were moved by one impulse and inspired by one soul." They looked like true soldiers.[88]

"This," remarked General Hooker, "is the famous fourth brigade." "Yes," rejoined the President, "it is commanded by the only Quaker General I have in the army."[89]

Captain James Stewart commanded Battery B, which was attached to the Iron Brigade. Stewart rode his horse, Tartar, in the review. When the ceremonies were over, Captain Stewart had a message: he was to report to the President. Mr. Lincoln spoke with the officer. However, Stewart was almost harassed, not by the President, but by Tad. Mr. Lincoln's son had been riding a pony. He had fallen in love with Captain Stewart's horse and wanted the artillery officer to swap horses, "Tartar for the pony." Tad kept saying, "My father is the President."[90]

FRIDAY, APRIL 10

This morning, Mr. Lincoln was still at Falmouth. Once again he was in the field, visiting the troops. The President reviewed O.O. Howard's Eleventh Corps and then the Twelfth Corps. Oliver O. Howard, the commander of the Eleventh Corps, was impressed with the review: "There was a column of about 70,000 men, and it must have taken over two and a half hours for them to pass the President.…Mrs. Lincoln came down from Washington, and the President's two sons were at the grand review. The smaller, Tad, rode a beautiful pony, and was noticeable for his ability to manage him."[91]

On this occasion, Howard was speaking of April 8, when the Second, Third, Fifth and Sixth Corps marched by the President. Then Howard noted that on April 10, "Mr. Lincoln came to review my troops. The German pioneers had fixed up my tent and its surroundings with everything that evergreens and trees could do to make them cheerful." Lincoln "took special notice and expressed his admiration."[92]

Justus M. Sillman of the Seventeenth Connecticut wrote to his family, "Abraham looked careworn and thin. He complimented the appearance of our corps through a circular from General Howard."[93]

William Wheeler was a member of the Thirteenth New York Battery. Wheeler was proud of "our old Eleventh Corps, and I doubt if the President has seen, in the whole Army of the Potomac, a hardier or more soldiery looking set of men. He rode past on a splendid black horse, followed by his two little boys, and then came an enormous and splendid cortege of at least two hundred officers."[94]

The log of the Eleventh Corps consists of these notations for those momentous days in April when Mr. Lincoln traveled to Virginia to meet with his generals and review the troops:

> *April 5: Rain & Snow. President Lincoln and lady arrive at Hdqrs A Pot. The band of the 33rd Mass Vols is sent to HdQrs.*
>
> *April 6: Cloudy & chilly. Cavalry was reviewed by the President near Gen. Birney HdQrs. The entire Cavalry of the Army of the Potomac is on the ground.*
>
> *April 7: Cloudy & cool. Hd Qrs of the Corps removed to the crossing of the corduroy and Railroad.*

April 8: Cool and cloudy. Gen Howard leaves Hd Qrs. The Pres of the U.S. reviews the 2nd, 3rd, 5th, & 6th Corps Army of the Potomac.

April 9. Cool & clear. 11 a.m. The President arrives at Hd Qrs. 12 p.m.: review of the 11th Corps by the President. 3 p.m. Review of the 12th Corps. 5 p.m. President leaves for Washington.

Mr. Lincoln also reviewed the Twelfth Corps, commanded by Henry Warner Slocum. The troops in the Twelfth Corps had served in the Shenandoah Valley under Nathaniel P. Banks, chasing Thomas J. Jackson in the famous Valley Campaign. Then, in September 1862, they were placed in the newly formed Twelfth Corps. The first commander was Joseph F.K. Mansfield. He held command for two days, being mortally wounded at Antietam at the edge of the East Woods.

Henry Warner Slocum was the commander in 1863. Henry graduated from West Point in 1852. For a while, he roomed with Philip Henry Sheridan at the Academy. He was severely wounded at First Bull Run. Edmund Brown of the Twenty-Seventh Indiana said of Slocum, "He was a quiet, retiring cultured gentleman, always unassuming and courteous…but firm and capable. At this time…he weighed about 150 pounds and was about thirty-five years old."[95]

Slocum did not talk about the review of the Twelfth Corps, but he received a bouquet of flowers from none other than Mrs. Mary Todd Lincoln. The question is why Slocum was the recipient. Secondly, his reaction is surprising. He had a flashback in time and remembered a gift of flowers from a young lady while he was attending the Albany State Normal School:

Headquarters, Twelfth Corps d'Armee,

April 19, 1863

My Dear Clara:
I received a beautiful bouquet this morning from Mary. The flowers are all from the President's garden. It is beautiful. The flowers are arranged according to color in three rows—red, white, and blue—with a fine japonica at the apex. I send you two or three samples.

I thought Mary would remember me. I take back all I have said unless she has sent to all other generals.

I do not think I was so happy over this bouquet of rare flowers from the wife of the President as I was over a single blue forget-me-not received by me while in Albany from a young country girl.

Yours affectionately,
H.W. Slocum[96]

General A.S. Williams, a division commander in the Twelfth Corps, continued his dedicated writing to his daughters back in Michigan:

Stafford Court House, April 14, 1863.

My Dear Daughter:
We have had ten days of such continuous reviews that I have hardly written a letter. The President and Mrs. Lincoln and family and a long string of satellites came down and spent a week or more, reviewing the troops. First, all the cavalry that could be spared from duty—over 12,000—were reviewed together, then the artillery, then four corps [probably 60,000] *infantry together, and then the other corps separately. Our corps was the last reviewed, as we are on the extreme right. We had difficulty in finding open ground enough in this broken and pine-barren country to get our two divisions into reviewing positions. As it was, we were obliged to mass each regiment by two-company fronts. But we made a very fine show, as the ground, from its undulating surface, gave a conspicuous and picturesque appearance to the masses moving over the crests and down the slopes.*

The President and Gen. Hooker were greatly fagged, as they had been almost every day on horseback for hours and had on that day reviewed one corps [Eleventh] *before ours. Mrs. Lincoln and other ladies came over (in spite of bad roads) in ambulances. I doubt if any week in the history of our country has ever witnessed such a large display of fine troops. The army never looked better and but for the small regiments in some corps would certainly impress one with its invincibility. If properly handled I feel that it must carry everything before it.*[97]

Edmund Brown and the members of the Twenty-Seventh Indiana were getting tired during the military reviews and the waiting. The troops would be formed and then stand in formation for hours until the brass arrived for the reviews.[98]

The men from Indiana had been in three major reviews since March 5. On that date, the Twelfth Corps had been reviewed by Generals Hooker and Slocum. That was the first time the men in the ranks really had the opportunity to observe the two generals. On March 18, there was another review, primarily for the benefit of General Hooker. Brown was not favorable. "He [Hooker] was nothing if not theatrical….He came amid the character dressing and other stage effects.…[There] was the thunderous roar of cannon, mounted upon his white stallion, moving like the wind, a hundred or more orderlies galloping at his heels. The whole cavalcade was gorgeous and resplendent in shining new uniforms." Brown was impressed by the sashes, banners, guidons and streamers fluttering in the March wind.[99]

Then came the Presidential review on April 10. Brown was very impressed by the proceedings:

Not to have given all the soldiers an opportunity to see the illustrious and beloved President Lincoln, while visiting the army, would have been a crime. Much as we all revered him, even then, and implicitly as we all believed in him, many of us never saw him before or afterwards. That sight alone almost compensated us for our entire service in the army. To have lived in his generation without seeing him would be a matter of lifelong regret. And the vision of his tall, angular form, his long, dangling legs, his pants working up and exposing his boot tops, his high silk hat bobbing up and down on his head, as he trotted by on horseback; and his plain, homely and sad, though noble, kindly and inspiring face, as it beamed upon us when we marched by him in review, will be fondly and proudly cherished by each of us, when the resounding salvos of artillery, the brilliant cavalcade of high officers and their retinues, the blare of bugles and the music of bands, the fluttering and drooping of flags and banners, the endless procession of marching and wheeling battalions of trained veterans, and the many other factors of that great and memorable pageant, have faded entirely out of mind.

The President had then the short, rather uneven whiskers that he seems to have worn during most, if not all, of his administration. Pictures of him were so common that any one of us would likely have known him anywhere. In that sense we were neither surprised nor disappointed by his appearance. In every respect, however, in which we had not heard about him, and in all those gifts and graces with which our youthful imagination, had endowed him, he measured more than up to the standard. Above all else, the evident fellow-feeling that he had for all true men, and his evident appreciation of the services we were trying to render the country, about which no one could be mistaken who saw him, greatly cheered and encouraged all of us. He seemed even more like "Father Abraham" to us after this than he had before.

The entire Twelfth Army Corps, its full quota of infantry, artillery, and the cavalry on duty with it, except the small numbers on other details, were present at this review.

And the details for the various necessary duties had been reduced as much as possible. The ground was sufficiently open and level, so that all were in sight at once. The occasion probably has the additional distinction, therefore, of being the largest number of soldiers any of us ever saw, at any one time.[100]

Mr. Lincoln had originally planned to stay with army for just a day. "But he found the visit was pleasant to the men and an agreeable respite from labor to him, and he prolonged his stay until he could visit all the corps of the army." He was concerned about the impending navy attack on Charleston and noted that "nothing could touch the tired spot within, which was all tired." Lincoln always spoke of the war as "this great trouble, just as a father might speak of a great domestic calamity."

We are indebted to Ward Hill Lamon for much of the information about Lincoln's visit to Antietam. For the first 1863 trip to Aquia Creek and Falmouth, Noah Brooks is the primary source of information. He summarized the great week in April in this manner:

The last review was held on April 10, when the Eleventh Corps, and the Twelfth Corps, were inspected.…The corps is now commanded by [Oliver O.] Howard, a gallant son of Maine who lost his right arm on the Peninsula. Carl Schurz has a division in this corps, and his brave Dutchmen are splendid soldiers, some of the best drilled…in the whole army.[101]

At last, the reviews were over, and the men in the ranks reflected. James Crole wrote to Hiram Averall in New York and said, "Father Abraham was here.…He visited all the camps in this vicinity he looks poor and careworn and appears as if he would not live to serve his time out.…I think his wife is not very good to him. He reminds me of a henpecked husband I seen once. I really feel sorry for the poor Rail Splitter for I have no doubt he is a good and honest man and means to do right if the vampires about him would let him alone."[102]

Daniel Holt, a physician, said, "Poor man, I pity him, and almost wonder at his being alive." Peter Welsh, a member of the Twenty-Eighth Massachusetts, wrote, "Old Abe was here he looks as though he would soon go to kingdom come."

A New York soldier noted, "The President looks very grave and worn; Mrs. Lincoln very fat and calm; and Master Lincoln very small and happy."

Charles Morse wrote, "Who would have thought, five years ago, that such a sight as this [the grand reviews] would ever be possible in democratic, republican America."[103]

Lieutenant George Breck said:

> *The President is probably one of the plainest appearing men in the country.*
> *He looks grave and worn, showing unmistakably the signs of vast care and*
> *responsibility that have so heavily borne and now rest upon him....What*
> *a tempest of duties, what a terrible ordeal of labor of mind and body....*
> *We must all admit that he has been placed in the most trying and onerous*
> *position that ever befell the lot of a President of the United States.*[104]

Along the Rappahannock

On Tuesday, May 5, 1863, the Virginia sky became cloudy and dark. At about 3:00 p.m., the rain started to fall. At first, it was only a shower, but then it fell in torrents. Rifle pits were filled with water. The soaked men bailed water until their backs stiffened. Roads became virtually impassable.

But in the midst of the storm, Joseph Hooker, commanding the Union army of the Potomac, gave the order to retreat from the Chancellorsville battle line. The corps commanders were shocked. They could not believe the order. The army had come to Chancellorsville in high hopes. Hooker had issued inspiring messages saying what he was going to do to the Confederates. However, Lee and Jackson had a surprise for him. And in the hour of opportunity, without committing half of his army, Hooker panicked. In a way, the rain was fitting. The storm marked the end of yet another sad story in the leadership in the Army of the Potomac.

The Rappahannock rose rapidly from the downpour and the ensuing flash flooding. Many Union soldiers, anxious to fight, hoped that the pontoons at the ford would be swept away. But despite the rising water and the stormy weather, the pontoons stayed in place. So the men, mules and wagons plowed through the mud and slid over the slippery roads.

Morale was low. The men had endured days of fatigue and hardship, and for what? Would they never get a leader? Alexander Webb said, "God pity our army." John Gibbon remarked, "I have lost all confidence in him [Hooker]." Many felt the same way. Hooker had been so popular. Now his troops treated him coolly, almost as if to say, "We have no further use for you."[105]

A cloud hung over the army. Officers and men tried to find someone on whom to place the blame and frustration. Darius Couch and Henry Warner Slocum were very outspoken in their criticism of Hooker; Couch, commanding the Second Corps, went so far as to say he could no longer serve under him. George G. Meade and John Fulton Reynolds agreed with the commanders of the Second and Twelfth Corps but were not as outspoken in their criticism.

Lincoln was also upset. He knew that a battle had occurred at Chancellorsville but received no dispatches until May 3. Then it was just a word from Daniel Butterfield, Hooker's chief of staff, saying that Hooker and Lee were engaged in battle. On Sunday, the third, Hooker finally sent a telegram that was quite evasive, saying that a battle had occurred resulting in "no success to us." He also criticized part of his army for not coming to his aid. He seemed confused.

On May 6 came the news that Hooker had recrossed the Rappahannock. President Lincoln turned white when he received the telegram. He walked back and forth with his hands clasped behind him, saying, "My God, my God what will the country say? What will the country say?"

Lincoln had received a telegram from Hooker on May 5, stating that the Confederates still held their positions in Fredericksburg. The next day, he called Assistant Secretary Fox to his office and instructed him to take copies of Richmond newspapers to Hooker's headquarters.

At 9:40 a.m. on the sixth, Lincoln telegraphed Hooker saying, "God bless you, and all with you. I know you will do your best." It seems that the President was still encouraging.

At 12:30 p.m., Lincoln sent another telegram to Hooker, stating that the Richmond papers had indeed admitted to the damage caused by Stoneman's cavalry raid. He also felt that the rains would prevent a Confederate flanking movement and that things were not as bad as they seemed.

At 4:30 p.m., Hooker sent the telegram relaying the information that the Army of the Potomac had indeed crossed the river and was on its way return to camp. Hooker said, "I saw no way of giving the enemy a general battle with the prospect of success."

Shortly thereafter, Lincoln was underway, headed for Falmouth and another conference with Joe Hooker. He took General Halleck with him. Earlier, during the visit of Senator Sumner from Massachusetts, he shared the story of yet another Union defeat, this time at Chancellorsville.

Arriving at Hooker's camp north of the Rappahannock, Lincoln and Halleck spent several hours talking with him. The President wanted to know the condition and morale of the army after the latest in the long series of defeats. So Mr. Lincoln summoned the corps commanders to a conference at Hooker's headquarters. The generals thought that Lincoln would ask questions about their feelings toward Hooker and the conduct of the battle. But the President said nothing. As a result, some of the generals were all in favor of sending a delegation to Lincoln asking for Hooker's removal. They decided against this channel largely because George Meade refused to go along with the idea.

The conversation with Hooker, as well as those with the other officers and men, occurred primarily on May 7. Lincoln heard defeat in their voices and saw it in their eyes. He returned to Washington in the evening.[106]

After Chancellorsville, it was just a matter of time before one of the two eastern armies moved on the opposing capital. With the defeat west of Fredericksburg and the low morale in the ranks of the officer corps and the soldiers, the Army of the Potomac was in no condition to strike again. It had to lick its wounds. And Lincoln had to find another commander.

Meanwhile, despite the loss of his right arm in Stonewall Jackson, Lee was in a better condition to move. His army began to think that it and its commander were invincible. And Lee thought that a victory in the North might bring an end to the war and final independence for the Confederate States of America. He wrote to Jefferson Davis advocating an invasion of the North.

In preparation, Lee reorganized and refitted the Army of Northern Virginia. The command was expanded to three corps. Jackson was gone. However, James Longstreet remained at the helm of the First Corps. Richard S. Ewell, an officer who had lost a leg at Second Manassas, was given command of the bulk of the corps formerly commanded by Jackson. A Third Corps was created, and A.P. Hill, a fiery light division leader, was assigned to the command.[107]

When the Army of Northern Virginia began its westward movement the first week in June, Colonel Ridden T. Bennett felt that it was "as tough an efficient as any army of the same number ever marshaled in this planet." Henry Heth, who would lead the opening action at Gettysburg, said, "There was not an officer or soldier in the Army of Northern Virginia…who did not believe that it was able to drive the Federal Army into the Atlantic Ocean." The exuberant *Richmond Whig* twitted that "an artificial leg ordered some months ago awaits General Ewell's arriving in the city of Philadelphia."[108]

The Army of Northern Virginia moved westward, crossed the mountains and used the mountains to shield the advance northward through the Shenandoah Valley. A Union garrison was swept aside during the Second Battle of Winchester, June 14–15, 1863. The next day, troops under command of Robert E. Rodes crossed the Potomac River at Williamsport.

The action at Winchester was so decisive that Ewell was being looked on as "another" Jackson. During the next ten days, the entire Confederate army crossed at Williamsport and at Shepherdstown Ford.

The Army of the Potomac crossed the river at Edwards Ferry on June 25–27. Leesburg was nearby on the southern bank of the river, while Poolesville, Maryland, was in front on the northern bank. Joseph Hooker and the army had to stay between Lee's army to the west and the cities of Baltimore and Washington to the east. Because of the road network, the Army of the Potomac made Frederick, Maryland, its objective.

Meanwhile, Confederate units had reached the south bank of the Susquehanna River. From the hills, they could look across and see Harrisburg, the capital of Pennsylvania. On June 29, Ewell's Confederate infantry was to march on Harrisburg from its position at Carlisle.[109]

Another Confederate column, led by John Gordon and William Smith, reached York, Pennsylvania. They reached the Susquehanna River east of York. They thought of marching on to Philadelphia, but the militia burned the bridge.

Lincoln and Halleck had had enough. Joe Hooker was not the answer. Thus, in the early morning hours of Sunday, June 28, with Harrisburg and Philadelphia being threatened by Robert E. Lee, Hooker was replaced. His successor was Pennsylvanian George Gordon Meade.

Late Sunday evening, a Confederate spy reached Chambersburg with the news that the Army of the Potomac was across the river and located in and around Frederick. There was the additional report that George Meade was the new commander.

Robert E. Lee issued a recall order. Looking at his map, he commanded the army to regroup at Cashtown or Gettysburg. Ewell was furious when he received his orders. He was ready to take Harrisburg. However, during the days of June 29–30, the two armies tramped through rain and mud, taking the roads of Maryland and Pennsylvania toward a Pennsylvania town by the name of Gettysburg; Meade's command moved on five roads like the fingers of a glove. He, too, was under orders to stay between the Army of Northern Virginia and the large cities of the east.

For three days in July, the battle to decide the fate of the nation raged around the little town of Gettysburg. The tide of battle swept back and forth on the slopes of Seminary and Cemetery Ridges. The blue and the gray fought to the death in the Peach Orchard, the Wheatfield and on the slopes of Little Round Top. Then on July 3 came Pickett's Charge, an assault of fifteen thousand primarily Virginia and North Carolina troops on the center of the Union Line held by Winfield Scott Hancock and others.

The massed flags of the Confederate regiments emerged from the woods on Seminary Ridge and crossed the open fields to the Emmittsburg Road, almost as though on parade. Then the Union guns opened. Before it was over, ten thousand or two-thirds of the attacking forces were killed, wounded or missing. The tide of the Confederacy crested at Gettysburg. Now slowly it began to recede.

On Seminary Ridge, Lee said, "Too bad. Too bad. It's all my fault." Orders were given for the army to withdraw by way of Hagerstown to the Potomac River.

Thousands of young men from the North and South had come to Gettysburg. Many never returned home to family and friends. Twenty-eight thousand men in the Army of Northern Virginia were casualties, along with twenty-three thousand in the Army of the Potomac. And in the fields and on the slopes of Little Round Top, Culp's Hill and other places, there were hundreds of blackened, bloated bodies needing decent burials.

The stench of death was in the air. Many had been buried in shallow graves or among the Confederates in vast trenches. A heavy rain came to wash the earth—perhaps to vent heaven's sorrow—on July 4 and 5. The coverings on many graves were washed away. At other places, hogs and wild animals rooted the bodies up and desecrated the graves. The *Adams Sentinel* for July 7 advertised, "Men, horses, wagons wanted immediately to bury the dead and to cleanse our streets."[110]

A few days after the battle, Pennsylvania's governor, Andrew Curtin, came to Gettysburg. He was appalled at the scenes of devastation. Something had to be done to ensure a decent burial for the valiant dead. Curtin appointed a prominent Gettysburg attorney, David Wills, to purchase land and create a fitting cemetery for the soldiers. The energetic Wills created a committee and went to work. Within three weeks, he had submitted a plan to Governor Curtin. By mid-August, fifteen of the seventeen governors of the Union states involved at the Gettysburg had pledged to assist in the project.

Meanwhile, David Wills and a prominent businessman in the area, David McConaughy, were in a dispute over land for the soldiers' cemetery. McConaughy was the owner of Evergreen Cemetery and had purchased adjoining land. By mid-August, Wills was also considering a proper service of dedication.

On August 28, 1863, Governor Curtin and Mr. Lincoln conversed at the White House. As a result, Curtin wrote to Wills about "the proper consecration of the grounds." The most important feature would be the main oration. For that task, none other than Edward Everett could be considered. The great orator was approached by the mayor of Boston. He replied that he could not possibly give the address prior to November 19. Thus, the date was set.

A few weeks later, on October 3, 1863, after continued prodding by Sarah Josepha Hale, Lincoln designated the last Thursday in November as a National Day of Thanksgiving.

As Wills proceeded with plans for the dedicatory events, Lincoln's friend Ward Hill Lamon was named to be marshal of the ceremonies consecrating the Soldiers' National Cemetery in Gettysburg.

On November 2, Judge Wills wrote an official invitation to Lincoln to attend the events scheduled for November 19. Wills also asked the President to share "a few appropriate remarks."

In the same mail, Wills sent a more personal note: "As the hotels in our town will be crowded…I write to invite you to stop with me.…Governor Curtin and Honorable Edward Everett will be my guests at the time and if you can come will you please join them at my house."

Many books and articles have been written on the Gettysburg Address. It is not our idea to go into much detail. However, some would say that Lincoln was invited as an afterthought. Some scholars note that Mr. Everett had more than two months to prepare his speech, while Lincoln had about two weeks.

GETTYSBURG, NOVEMBER 18–19

One week before the dedicatory events, Ward Hill Lamon and his top aide, Benjamin B. French, went by rail to Gettysburg to check on all the preparations. They checked in at the Eagle Hotel and went over the program for November 19. The weather turned colder, and when Lamon and French returned to Washington on November 14, they were met by a thunderstorm bringing another cold front to the capital.

While Lamon was in Gettysburg, Lincoln attended the social event of the year in Washington: the wedding of Kate Chase, the daughter of the secretary of the treasury. Kate was politically ambitious, intelligent and shrewd. She was also beautiful and the belle of Washington. The President attended alone, as Mrs. Lincoln detested "Miss C," as she called Kate. She had instructed Abe not to speak to her at the receptions because she was deceitful. He had to attend because Kate was the daughter of a cabinet member. She married the wealthy William Sprague, former governor and, in 1863, a senator from Rhode Island. Mr. Lincoln did not tarry at the reception. He returned to the White House quickly. He had one more week until the big day in Gettysburg.

The public had been informed by the media of the Gettysburg events on November 7. Two days later, Mr. Lincoln went to Ford's Theatre and sat in the box he usually occupied. The performance starred John Wilkes Booth in *The Marble Heart*.

Always considerate of others, Mr. Lincoln made two trips, both on Sunday, November 8 and 15. On the first, he went with his secretaries Nicolay and Hay to the Photographic Gallery of Alexander Gardner. He went again a week later with his friend Noah Brooks. Mr. Lincoln went to Gardners on Sunday so he would not disturb Mr. Gardner's regular photographic business.[111]

On the seventeenth, Mr. Lincoln watched a parade in Washington. The occasion was the march of 2,500 members of the Invalid Corps. The President attended a cabinet meeting and discussed travel arrangements for Gettysburg. Secretary Stanton had scheduled a one-day trip, but Lincoln did not like the arrangement. "I do not wish to so go that by the slightest accident we fail entirely, and at the best, the whole be a mere breathless running of the gauntlet." During the evening, he examined a drawing of the burial plot of the National Cemetery at Gettysburg. Lincoln also told Joshua Speed that he had about half of his Gettysburg speech prepared.

The eighteenth did not dawn very well. Mr. Lincoln was feeling a little ill. Worse yet, ten-year-old Tad had suddenly taken sick. After Willie's death, this was very threatening. Mrs. Lincoln grabbed the President's arm and begged, "Don't go. Stay home with Tad and me." She became hysterical. This time, the President did not yield to her behavior. He had made a commitment to go to Gettysburg. And go he must, even though he was not feeling well and Tad was ill. About noon, the President departed on a special four-car train provided by the Baltimore and Ohio Railroad. His personal secretaries, Nicolay and Hay, were on board. So were members of the diplomatic corps, the Invalid Corps and the U.S. Marine Band.

Traveling with Mr. Lincoln to Gettysburg were three cabinet members: Secretary of State William Seward, Secretary of the Interior John Palmer Usher and Postmaster General Montgomery Blair.

Seward, from New York, had been a political opponent in 1860. However, Lincoln valued his knowledge, tact and friendship and relied heavily on the former senator. Usher, a lawyer and former attorney general from Indiana, was an old friend. In earlier days, Usher and Lincoln had ridden the Eighth Circuit in Illinois. Blair, known as "Monty" to his friends, was a tall man with an erect military bearing. He was the best-educated member of the cabinet.

His father, Francis P. Blair, had been Andrew Jackson's ghostwriter and one of the founding fathers of the Republican Party. Lincoln had turned to the Blairs in an effort to keep Maryland and Missouri in the Union, and the elder Blair had sought in vain to persuade Robert E. Lee to accept command of the Union armies in the spring of 1861.

The trip to Baltimore took seventy minutes. At exactly 1:10 p.m., the train slowed at Baltimore's B&O Bolton Street Station. Two babies were presented to Mr. Lincoln by their adoring mothers. He kissed the little ones.[112]

The cars were unhitched and pulled by horses to the Calvert Street Station of the North Central Railroad. A windowless baggage car was added and placed between the third car and the one containing the President. A Baltimore lad, Andrew B. Staley, became the news and candy boy for the next leg of the journey to Gettysburg.

By 2:00 p.m., the newly constituted train was ready to pull out. A few moments prior to departure, General James F. Schenck, a wounded veteran of Bull Run, boarded the train along with his staff.

During the fifty-mile trip to Hanover Junction, the President and his guests ate lunch at a long table set up in the converted baggage car. Mr. Lincoln ate little because he wasn't feeling very well. No doubt his speech and thoughts of the sick Tad were on his mind.

Hanover Junction was a hamlet. However, there was a general store and a blacksmith shop. At the junction, the Presidential train was to link up with the Governor's Special, the train carrying Governor Curtin and the dignitaries from Harrisburg. However, there was a major delay.

At Hanover Junction, there was another switch. The train and a new engine changed to the Hanover Branch Railroad. Then the Gettysburg Special made the twenty-four-mile run to Hanover. Most of the town was out to greet Mr. Lincoln and those in his group. The crowd received an unexpected treat when, expecting to see just the train, an eastbound train forced the President's train to actually halt for eight minutes.

Reverend M.J. Alleman came on board and greeted the President, "Father Abraham, your children want to see you." Students of the Gettysburg trip note that this was a poor way to begin the conversation with the President, who disliked that term as well as "Mr. President." He was very informal. Lincoln made a few comments. Ladies came forward and gave him flowers as well as a lovely flag. The colors were the work of their hands. The flag was placed in the rear of the Presidential car.

Then the train pulled out. It was on the last leg of the journey to Gettysburg. Some say that Lincoln sat and thought and jotted notes. Earlier, he had determined that in his brief remarks, he would not mention a single person, nor the battle itself. Instead, he would deal with the larger issues: sacrifice, commitment and the "unfinished task" before the people. The train moved on. White smoke belched from the stack. Sparks flew out along the railroad right of way. At crossings, or when people were seen along the route, the bell was rung. The cars jolted along on the track. Travel by train was not the most comfortable method of getting from place to place.[113]

It was now about 6:00 p.m. Darkness had fallen across the land. However, Gettysburg was filled to capacity. In July, the city and surrounding countryside had been filled with the troops of the blue and gray. Now there were people everywhere, coming for the dedication of the soldiers' cemetery. A large crowd was gathered at the Carlisle Street Railroad Depot waiting for the train from Washington.

The town had been founded by James Getty in 1780. Many of the settlers were Scotch-Irish. And city was the seat of government for Adams County, Pennsylvania. By 1860, the population had grown to 2,300. Gettysburg was also a major manufacturing city, producing well-built carriages—ten small businesses were devoted to that endeavor. Gettysburg was also important for education. Pennsylvania College (now Gettysburg College) was located in the town, as was the Lutheran Theological Seminary, standing on the ridge that bears its name. There was also a school for young ladies.

As the train chugged to a halt, there were cheers. However, on the station platform there were grim reminders of the days in July in the form of piled coffins.

Pushing their way through the crowd was Lincoln's old reliable friend Ward Hill Lamon and the Honorable David Wills. Edward Everett was also present, as was General Darius Couch. The next objective was to reach the Square or "Diamond," one hundred yards or so to the south. Soldiers sought to make a pathway for the President. En route, hundreds of admiring people thrusts their hands between the ranks in an effort to touch Mr. Lincoln.[114]

Dinner was at the Wills home. Two dozen guests were there, including a French diplomat and an admiral. Edward Everett, the featured speaker for the next day, was also present. Everett had met Mr. Lincoln shortly before the 1861 inauguration. He noted in his journal that Lincoln "is not a person of uncouth appearance and manners, but as a peer of any man at the table."

Lincoln, perhaps preoccupied by the war and Tad's illness, excused himself a little early. He took with him William Slade, his valet, at about 10:00 p.m. Lincoln sent Slade for Secretary Seward, whom he wanted to review his speech.

Seward was not at the Wills house. He was next door at the home of Robert G. Harper. Lincoln walked over to see the secretary. The crowds still thronged the streets. Sergeant Paxton Bingham had to run interference for the President. There was no Secret Service.

Seward and Lincoln discussed the address. At about 11:00 p.m., they were joined by Pennsylvania's Governor Andrew Curtin. The train had been delayed by heavy rail traffic. Judge Wills was embarrassed because he had failed to make reservations for Governor Curtin.

Like press secretaries today, John Hay, Lincoln's private secretary, was hounded by the press, seeking to determine the content of the Presidential address. Young John probably knew that Mr. Lincoln had been preparing for this speech all his life. Many of the phrases he would use he had quoted as one-liners in previous speeches.

After a while, Lincoln returned to his second-floor bedroom, overlooking the Gettysburg Town Square. Bands continued to play outside, and the large crowd clamored for a speech. He made a few remarks and then begged off, saying he had nothing else prepared. Mr. Lincoln did not like to speak off the cuff or without prepared notes.

Sometime after midnight, on November 19, Mr. Lincoln went to bed. No one knows what was on his mind. However, his sleep may have been a little more peaceful because of a message that there was no news from the battlefront, and his beloved Tad was also feeling a little better. Beneath his window, in the Diamond, the crowd continued to sing, "We Are Coming, Father Abraham."

Sleep may have been a little more difficult for Ward Hill Lamon. He had met with more than seventy marshals during the evening. Hill, as Lincoln called him, was in charge of crowd control and the timing of the events. Lamon knew that he had a major task.

Dawn came to Adams County and was greeted at 7:00 a.m. by artillery salvos fired from Cemetery Hill. The nation and the world already knew about the Battle of Gettysburg. It would soon be ranked among the most decisive engagements of all time. But before the day was over, Gettysburg would have additional fame, in the words of inspiration and strength embodying the thoughts of Lincoln and the nation.

The roads were full of horse-drawn vehicles carrying passengers into Gettysburg. Periodically, trains arrived at the depot, with countless others coming for the ceremonies. The aroma of coffee and bacon and smoke from stoves filled the air. Flags were everywhere, and by midmorning people were taking their places in second-story windows for choice seats.

Gettysburg Train Station. *Pictures of Us, Pennsylvania, pennsylvania.picturesofus.net.*

Details of Mr. Lincoln's early morning activities are scarce. He apparently wanted to see some of the battlefield but changed his mind after seeing the throngs of people. John Nicolay went to his room at 9:00 a.m. and recalled that the President had made a new copy of his speech. At about the same time, Sergeant Bingham was relieved from his guard duty. James A. Rebert, Company B, Twenty-First Pennsylvania Cavalry, assumed the post of guarding the President. At about 10:00 a.m., Mr. Lincoln placed his two pages of notes in his pocket and put on white gloves. Then he went downstairs to join the procession.[115]

At the doorway of the Wills house, Lincoln placed his hand on the shoulder of the twelve-year-old son of Governor Curtin and then stepped outside into the noise and confusion of midmorning. Lamon and the marshals had tried to get one hundred horses into the Diamond for the dignitaries to ride to the cemetery.

The President walked through a pathway made by soldiers to a small bay horse. Those who selected the animal had not considered Lincoln's height. The bay was too small, and the President's legs almost touched the ground.

Gettysburg Presbyterian Church. *Pictures of Us, Pennsylvania, pennsylvania.picturesofus.net.*

The plans for the day had been carefully orchestrated. However, the crowds and problems were greater than had been anticipated. Lamon was trying to get the guests in proper order, according to protocol. Many paid little attention to him. They were caught up in the atmosphere of the moment. Poor Mr. Lincoln sat on the bay for one hour. And all that time people were coming up to greet him and shake his hand.

While he sat on his horse in the Diamond, a message was handed to him. Secretary Stanton had sent a communiqué from General Grant stating that a battle was not imminent. There was also another report about Tad. The little fellow was better—"he will be out today." At that, Lincoln smiled. Now he could give his undivided attention to his remarks.

At about 11:00 a.m., nearly one hour later, the procession began to move south on Baltimore Street. The crowd surged forward. Leading the procession was the United States Marine Band, followed by military units, generals, distinguished guests and then, in a reminder of the epic battle, the wounded veterans; civilians followed. Every minute, a cannon shot resounded across the Pennsylvania hills.

Lincoln held the reins of his horse, smiled from time to time and occasionally waved to the people. But he seemed lost in thought. Along the route, a little girl was given to Mr. Lincoln. He gave her a short ride, kissed her on the forehead and then returned her to her parents. A horse behind Lincoln became interested in the bay's tail and had to be restrained from nipping it.

It didn't take long to reach the cemetery. It was difficult to get through the crowd to reach the speaker's platform. It was small, about twelve by twenty feet. The President dismounted and was ushered through the crowd. When he reached the platform and the throng caught a glimpse of him, they cheered. Lincoln was placed on an old settee between Secretary Seward and Mr. Everett.

The ceremonies began as Brigfield's Band of Philadelphia played a dirge. Then Reverend Mr. Stockon, chaplain of the senate, offered the invocation. Some say that the prayer was itself an oration. Then it was time for the main event, the oration by Edward Everett. He spoke for one hour and fifty-seven minutes.

Among those present at the dedicatory ceremonies were General John Gibbon and his aide, Lieutenant Frank Haskell. Gibbon was recovering from wounds he had received on July 3. He and Haskell grew tired of Everett's long oration and strolled south on Cemetery Ridge to the positions the Second Corps occupied during the battle. Gibbon noted, "We then returned in time to hear Mr. Lincoln's touching address."[116]

When the distinguished orator completed his remarks, Mr. Lincoln stood and joined in the applause. The President grasped his hand and said, "I am grateful." Seward then placed a blanket around the exhausted speaker.

Some of the folks had wandered off during the long speech. But now they returned to the edge of the crowd. They wanted to hear what was coming next. First, though, there was a five-stanza dirge by the Baltimore Glee Club. Among the words written by Benjamin French were "Tis holy ground—This spot where, in their graves, We place our Country's brave, Who fell in Freedom's holy cause."

As the sound of song faded away, Ward Hill Lamon, a big man, strode forward from his position near the platform. He stood even larger on this day, as he had a distinct honor. In fact, Hill said, it was one of the great moments of his life. With a loud, ringing voice, Ward Hill Lamon almost shouted, "The President of the United States."

Flags hung limply. There was no breeze. Lincoln laid his gray shawl aside and placed his wire-rimmed glasses on his nose. He rose, and the floor creaked beneath his feet. He held the two pages of his remarks in his hand. He gazed at the crowd, looking at individuals, thinking of America and giving himself time to gain complete composure. Then he gazed at the "Stars and Stripes" hanging limply on the main pole.

Placing one hand on his lapel, he began to speak. He had a high-pitched voice and enjoyed speaking outdoors. He spoke very slowly, emphasizing each word and thought. He glanced at his notes but once. At one point, when he spoke of "under God," his voice almost broke.

Thirty-two-year-old Charles Hale, a nephew of Edward Everett and a member of the Massachusetts delegation, carefully noted the entire address in shorthand. In just about two minutes, Lincoln completed his "few appropriate remarks," consisting of just 271 words. He went back to his seat. Some say there was applause; others state there was silence. Lincoln thought he had failed.

Later, some papers wrote about the nonsense of the speech. Others said, "It was brief and beautiful." And Edward Everett told the President, "I should be glad if I could flatter myself that I came as near the central idea of the occasion in two hours, as you did in two minutes."

Dr. Baugher, the president of Gettysburg College, pronounced the benediction. The dedication of the Soldiers' National Cemetery was over. The crowd began to disperse. Lincoln and the other dignitaries were escorted to the home of Judge Wills. There was a large reception. Mr. Lincoln shook hands with thousands of the rank and file—"we the people."

The President had also heard the story of old John Burns, the cobbler who had grabbed his squirrel gun and joined the Union infantry to fight the Confederates on July 1. Burns had been wounded several times. Mr. Lincoln wanted to meet him.

John Burns responded to the Presidential invitation wearing the same clothes in which he had done battle with members of Lee's army—bullet holes and all. After conversing a bit, Lincoln and Burns walked arm in arm to the Presbyterian church. The sanctuary had served as a hospital for the wounded of the Union First Corps and many others during the battle. Lincoln and Burns sat in the second pew, listening to a talk by Charles Anderson, the man chosen to be the next vice-governor of Ohio. Charles was a brother to the defender and hero of Fort Sumter, Major Robert Anderson. His message was far different from the one uttered by Lincoln in the cemetery. The tone of the message was that of revenge—those who had gone to war from the South were traitors.[117]

Before Anderson finished, Lincoln had to go. He had to meet his train. The President shook hands and then left the church.

All trains were held up until the President departed at 6:30 p.m. He was not feeling well. In fact, he stretched out on a bed of chairs. He had a severe headache. This was the onset of the mild case of smallpox that would slow the President for the next two weeks.

During most of the trip, the President remained in solitude. However, at Hanover Junction, Wane McVeagh, a prominent Republican leader, had to leave the train. He had been one of the few to congratulate the President after his remarks at Gettysburg. Before leaving the train, McVeagh said, "I can only say that the words you spoke will live in the land's language."

As the train continued toward Baltimore and Washington, the President rested. Since Antietam, when disparaging remarks had been written about laughing and joking in the presence of the wounded and burial parties, he had wanted to tell the nation what he thought of "the terrible cruel war." That opportunity had come. He who carried the burden of the nation had spoken from a lifetime of experience. He had spoken from his heart and the depth of his being. Soon his words spoken at Gettysburg would be wafting on the wings of time with eternal truths of politics and history. Abraham Lincoln had never stood taller or spoken more eloquently than that Thursday afternoon in Pennsylvania. The world would indeed long "remember what they had heard on the fields of Pennsylvania"—and likewise "long remember" the words of Lincoln.[118]

An Autumn afternoon,
Mid November,
Throngs of people.
Music, a parade,
Dirges, prayers,
A long oration.
Then a tall thin, man,
Speaking from deep within,
A few appropriate remarks,
Only 271 words.
Mr. Lincoln,
Gettysburg,
November 19, 1863.
And those who were there
Had seen and heard history
Being made.

—*John W. Schildt*

Point Lookout, Maryland

Thousands of Confederate prisoners were taken at Gettysburg. The federal government needed a large prisoner of war camp. The site selected was at Point Lookout, the southern tip of Maryland, with the Potomac River on one side and the Chesapeake Bay on the other.

At the end of December 1863, Mr. Lincoln made his last journey of the eventful year. On the twenty-sixth, he wrote to Secretary Stanton about leaving from the wharf and perhaps taking Mrs. Lincoln and Tad with him.

Lincoln and Secretary Stanton traveled to Point Lookout. There they conferred with General Marston and viewed the prisoners of war. Mr. Lincoln and the secretary of war spent the night and then returned to Washington on December 28.

By the end of the war, more than twenty thousand Confederates had been incarcerated at Point Lookout. About four thousand, 20 percent, died during their confinement. Many were buried in unmarked graves. Today, there are many ghost stories associated with the site. The record at Point Lookout rivals that of the notorious Andersonville Prison of the Confederacy. It is now a Maryland State Park. Extensive archaeological work was done and revealed many interesting artifacts.

St. Mary's County was closely linked to the Confederacy. The people were in sympathy with the cause of the South. Items were smuggled across the Potomac into Virginia.

Lincoln's visit to Point Lookout was supposedly made in an effort to get the captured Confederates to renounce their loyalty to the South and affirm their support for the Union.

An article by Jason Babacock in the *Southern Maryland News* of April 22, 2009, noted that federal funds would be used to repair the monument to the Confederates who died at Point Lookout.[119]

TRAVELS IN 1864

Baltimore

The tide of the Confederacy crested first at Antietam and then again the following summer at Gettysburg. However, with the retreat to Virginia, many in the South realized that it was just a matter of time until the superior manpower and supplies of the North would triumph.

Lincoln took a step to ensure this reality when, in March 1864, he placed U.S. Grant in charge of all the Union armies. Grant came east and moved with the Army of the Potomac. When the spring of 1864 arrived, the army crossed the Rapidan and moved toward the tangled underbrush of a wooded area called the Wilderness, west of Fredericksburg. During May 5–6, Grant suffered heavy losses. He could replace his men; Lee couldn't. The woods caught fire, and some of the wounded burned to death. When the fighting died down, the Confederates expected Grant to follow the path of the rest of the Union generals and retreat toward Washington. Late that night, they heard sounds. Grant was not retreating. Instead, he was heading south. Lee placed his army in motion also, and in mid-May, battles raged around Spotsylvania Court House. Trees were cut down by bullets, and one section of the battlefield became known as the Bloody Angle.

Again Grant headed south, and for several weeks, Lee, with the interior lines, kept one step ahead of Grant, until they reached the confines of Petersburg. There Grant kept extending his lines, and each extension depleted the ranks of the Army of Northern Virginia.

Between the Battles of the Wilderness and Spotsylvania Court House, Mr. Lincoln made two trips of a nonpolitical nature. On April 17, 1864, the President received an invitation from William J. Albert, president of the Maryland Sanitary Fair, to be his guest at the opening of a fair designed to raise funds in Baltimore.

The United States Sanitary Commission was a vital part of the war effort. The concept had been inspired by the deeds of the British Sanitary Commission during the Crimean War. In 1861, many groups, composed mostly of women, sprang up across the land. Their goal was to support the troops in the field—to do for the soldiers "what the government could not do." This included preparing kits that included hygienic items, combs, needles and perhaps additional socks. Occasionally, both the soldiers in the field and the wounded received packages of food and other needed items. Women and later older men went to the hospitals, compiled lists of the sick and wounded and wrote letters home for the soldiers unable to write. They assisted the wounded in finding transportation home and also temporary housing in some cities.

The primary group was the Women's Central Association of Relief in Metropolitan New York. Dr. Henry W. Bellows was instrumental in bringing the various relief groups together. The result was the United States Sanitary Commission, the forerunner of the American Red Cross.

Mr. Lincoln responded immediately to the request from Mr. Albert. He boarded a train on April 18 and headed northeast to Baltimore. Three years earlier, he had entered the city in secrecy, as there were supposed threats on his life. Massachusetts troops arriving in April 1861 were stoned, and Baltimore was considered a "Hotbed of Secession." This time, things were vastly different.

Philadelphia

Less than two months later, on June 15, Mr. Lincoln and a group of compatriots departed from Washington on a special train. It was early, 7:00 a.m. They were going to Philadelphia to attend the Great Central Fair in aid of the U.S. Sanitary Commission. Brief stops were made in Baltimore and Wilmington. The train arrived in Philadelphia at about 11:30 a.m. Mr. Lincoln was escorted to the Continental Hotel.

After lunch, the Presidential party traveled to the Logan Square fairgrounds. They arrived at about 4:15 p.m. During the banquet in the main assembly hall, Lincoln responded to a toast:

War, at the best, is terrible, and this war of ours, in its magnitude and in its duration, is one of the most terrible.

...It has destroyed property, and ruined homes....We accepted this war for an object, a worthy object, and the war will end when the object is obtained....I have never been in the habit of making predictions in regard to the war, but I am almost tempted to make one. If I were to hazard it, it is this: That Grant is this evening with General Meade and General Hancock, of Pennsylvania, and the brave officers and soldiers with him, in a position from whence he will never be dislodged until Richmond is taken.[120]

Following the President's remarks, Major General Lew Wallace, Edward Everett and others spoke. Several gifts were given to the President, including a silver medal from the ladies of the fair. The President graciously accepted the gifts.

Then Mr. Lincoln departed the fairgrounds for the Union League Club. He was escorted in a torchlight procession. He spoke briefly at the club in response to a welcome by Daniel Dougherty, a prominent Philadelphia lawyer. After the reception, he spoke again from the balcony:

I attended the Fair at Philadelphia today in the hope that I might aid something in swelling the contributions for the benefit of the soldiers in the field....I thought I might do this without impropriety.[121]

Mr. Lincoln went on to say that he had not expected the demonstration of the group; he had not come for that purpose and seemed surprised. He appeared on the balcony simply to say "thanks" and to share gratitude and respect "for the demonstration in my honor." Earlier, the President had turned down an invitation to attend a program at the Arch Street Theater. At 8:00 a.m. on June 17, Lincoln and his party departed Philadelphia, heading back to his tasks in Washington.

Mr. Lincoln needed the trip to Philadelphia. He had not lost faith in U.S. Grant. He was a general who fought, a commander who kept nipping at Lee's heel and would not let go. However, Union losses in Virginia were staggering. By June 12, Grant had inflicted heavy losses on the Army of Northern Virginia. These were men the Confederacy could not replace. However, in the engagement in the Wilderness, at Spotsylvania and Cold Harbor, Grand had lost fifty-four thousand men. The people in the North were tired of war, and they had grave questions about the commander they called "Butcher Grant."

However, Grant had modern ideas. He realized the importance of supplies and logistics. He set his sights on Petersburg, a city of eighteen thousand southeast of Richmond, as well as an important rail and road terminus. Four rail lines carried supplies into Petersburg and thence to Richmond. Grant proposed to cut the Confederate supply line from Petersburg to Richmond. Grant was ready to begin his approach to total warfare. Petersburg was "the jugular vein of the Confederacy," and he was going for it.

Petersburg was officially created in 1748. The city suffered extensively during the Revolutionary War, when it was occupied by British troops commanded by Generals William Phillips and Benedict Arnold. Tragedy struck again in 1815. At that time, a raging fire consumed four hundred buildings. By 1861, Petersburg had been rebuilt and had reached a place of prominence. It was a railroad, flour and tobacco center.

Now, like many other places in history, it had the misfortune to be in the path of contending armies—a place of strategic importance. As Grant moved toward Petersburg in June 1864, the city would be slowly strangled. Frequently, Petersburg was shelled by Union artillery, yet there were very few civilian casualties over the next ten months. Economic and living conditions became quite bad for the residents, and by the spring of 1865, about thirteen thousand of the eighteen thousand residents had fled as refugees.

Military history often hinges on moments and miles. The Union Eighteenth Corps reached the Petersburg front on June 15. The commander was very cautious and delayed his attack. Later in the day, the Union Second Corps arrived on the scene. Until the evening, Petersburg could have been taken rather easily. A rare opportunity was lost, for never again would Petersburg be as weakly defended as it was on the evening of June 15, 1864. "If the city had fallen in mid-June the siege and losses of ten months would have been averted."[122] Five days later, Lee became aware of Grant's intentions and began to entrench. And by July 9, Grant had begun to seriously consider entrenchments and fortifications leading to siege operations.

City Point

On June 15, Grant established his headquarters at City Point, Virginia. He would be close to the operations at Petersburg. City Point was a hamlet at the terminus of the City Point Railroad. Almost overnight, the rural area was transformed. City Point was located at the junction of the James and Appomattox Rivers. By water, it was within easy reach of Fort Monroe and Washington, D.C. City Point quickly became the scene of the greatest logistical operation of the Civil War. Railroads and telegraph lines were installed to link the Union armies in the field.

Grant established his headquarters on the front lawn of Dr. Richard Eppes's Appomattox Manor. The land had been in the Eppes family for many generations. Francis Eppes had received 1,700 acres as a land patent in 1635. Part of the manor house was constructed prior to the Revolutionary War. This was the center portion. The east and west wings were added prior to the Civil War.

Dr. Richard Eppes preferred farming to the practice of medicine. He served briefly in the Third Virginia Cavalry and then moved to Petersburg as a contract surgeon. Then came June 1864, U.S. Grant and the huge supply depot. Appomattox Manor remained in the Eppes family until obtained by the U.S. government in 1975.

Over the next nine months, Appomattox Manor and City Point was transformed. It became the supply line for 100,000 Federal soldiers. At first, tents were pitched everywhere. But as summer turned to autumn, and with the arrival of winter, wooden barracks and huts were constructed. Thousands of civilians were employed between June 16, 1864, and March 31, 1865, to build railroads, warehouses, barracks and offices. City Point was a bustling place.

C.L. McAlpine, an engineer, supervised the construction of twenty-one miles of railroad. This was the longest line built for military use in the war. The rails connected the warehouses, barracks and hospitals.

McAlpine's Construction Company erected 280 buildings to serve the military. It also built eight wharves to handle the constant arrival of ships. The smallest wharf was one by the name of Mail. It contained 11,340 square feet. The largest dock was Captain Camp's Wharf, consisting of 113,980 square feet. This was named for the assistant quartermaster responsible for clothing. For a while, City Point was one of the world's busiest seaports. Normally, there were forty steamships, seventy-five sailing vessels and one hundred barges anchored at the mile-long waterfront facility.

The Quartermaster Department was responsible for storage, transportation and distribution of supplies for the men and animals. Warehouses held twenty days' worth of forage for horses and mules, as well as a thirty-day supply of rations for the soldiers. Containers of beef, pork, bread, flour, vegetables, fruit, coffee, tea, sugar, salt, candles and soap arrived almost daily. It was big business. For instance, six hundred tons of hay and grain arrived daily.

Offices were constructed for the various departments. There was a harbormaster, a forage master, a railroad dispatcher and various other key persons. One of the largest bakeries in the nation turned out fresh bread for the troops.

Hospital facilities were prepared to care for ten thousand sick and wounded. This was one mile west of City Point. There were also stables, chapels, a post office and the "Bull Pen," a military prison capable of handling four hundred men, with the provost marshal in charge.

Communication with Washington and generals at the front was very important. It was a key element in the hands of Major General Rufus Ingals, chief quartermaster of "the armies closing in on Richmond and Petersburg." The telegraph office was in the first-floor bedroom of Appomattox Manor.

Lincoln saw the beginning of City Point's growth in the summer of 1864 and then spent two weeks on the *River Queen* just off City Point. Like most places connected with history, it was a little, obscure place until fate and history elevated it to national prominence. City Point was "the Southern Terminus of Northern Abundance." From June until April 1865, City Point was the supply depot for the Siege of Petersburg, the longest siege ever to occur on this continent.

City Point was not only the supply depot of the Army of the Potomac but the nerve center as well. Grant's headquarters was located on a bluff overlooking the James and Appomattox Rivers. During his ten-month stay, he made frequent visits to the front to visit the troops for inspections and, like a good commander, to be seen by the soldiers. At least five times during his stay at City Point, Grant traveled elsewhere. Twice he journeyed to visit Phil Sheridan and plot strategy. On two other occasions, Grant went to visit his wife in Burlington, New Jersey; the fifth trip was to Fort Fisher, North Carolina.

While Mr. Lincoln was in Philadelphia, the wily Lee was conceiving another brilliant plan to relieve the pressure on Petersburg and threaten Washington. Lee derived a scheme that would send Jubal Early's troops from the lines at Petersburg westward to Lynchburg. They would clear the Union forces there and then head northward into the Shenandoah Valley, cross the Potomac River, threaten Washington and, if possible, endeavor to release the thousands of Confederate soldiers imprisoned at Point Lookout. It was another bold and daring plan. Many of the Confederate troops selected for the operation had been a part of Stonewall Jackson's famed "foot cavalry." If any commander was capable of succeeding in such an operation, it was "Old Jube."

If Early could successfully complete his assignment, the South could still conceivably win the war. The defenses of Washington had been depleted. Grant had drawn men from the fortifications to aid in the Siege of Petersburg. Lee needed a bold stroke, and he needed it immediately. However, Lincoln also had some military thoughts. On June 20, he embarked on another wartime travel to City Point. Mr. Lincoln left Washington at 5:00 p.m. on the USS *Baltimore*. He took Tad and Assistant Secretary Gustavus Fox with him. The purpose was to meet with General Grant and briefly visit the army on the James River.[123]

The *Baltimore* arrived at City Point at about noon. Grant and his staff boarded the ship. Once again, Mr. Lincoln had health problems, "an upset stomach." Someone suggested a sip of champagne might help. With his keen wit, the President replied, "No thanks. Too many fellows get seasick ashore from drinking that very stuff."

Lincoln rested briefly and then went to Grant's headquarters. There he mounted the general's horse, Cincinnati, one of Grant's favorites. The President visited some of the troops in the lines near Petersburg. Grant rode his other horse, Jeff Davis. Mr. Lincoln also reviewed some of the black troops under General Edward Hincks. He received hearty cheers. The evening was most memorable.

Lincoln and Grant relaxed, sitting in front of the headquarters tent swapping stories. The President and his commanding general had a good relationship. He held Grant in high esteem. Lincoln once said that Grant was one of the few generals who never criticized him or blamed others for military problems. He fought and took the blame and shared the glory with others.

A great opportunity was missed by Mathew Brady. He had arrived in the area and was but eight miles away taking pictures of various generals, unaware that President Lincoln was visiting General Grant.

On June 22, the President and General Grant steamed up the James River to observe troop positions and visit the flagship of Rear Admiral Lee. En route, they picked up General Benjamin Butler at Bermuda Hundred and went up the river as far as it was considered safe. At 2:00 p.m., Butler and Lincoln returned to City Point on board the *Greyhound*. Then Lincoln departed on board the USS *Baltimore* for Washington. The group arrived at the Navy Yard at 5:00 p.m. the next day.

Meanwhile, Jubal Early was moving. He had been given his orders to threaten Washington and had departed the Petersburg area for Lynchburg on June 13. Brushing aside the Union forces under David Hunter, the Confederate column moved northward to Lexington. The Southern officers were filled with rage when they saw the Virginia Military Institute, burned and looted by Hunter's men. The column reversed muskets as it marched by the flower-strewn grave of Stonewall Jackson. Some shed tears. Another day's march brought Early's forces to Staunton. Former vice president John C. Breckinridge, from Kentucky, was named Early's chief lieutenant.

By July 2, the Confederates had reached Winchester. The next task was to disrupt the traffic of the Baltimore and Ohio Railroad in Martinsburg. By the fourth, Union forces had retreated to Harpers Ferry, and "Old Jube" was crossing the Potomac River at Shepherdstown. Moving then via Turner's, Fox's and Crampton's Gaps, the Confederate army proceeded toward Frederick.

July was characteristically a bad month for the Union. On July 21, 1861, there was the debacle at First Bull Run. July 1862 brought McClellan's withdrawal from the peninsula. The year 1863 was brighter, as there were major Union victories at Gettysburg and Vicksburg.

Now there was another threat. Braxton Bragg had advised Jefferson Davis, "It seems to me that this force [Hunter's] should be expelled from the Valley. If it could be crushed, Washington would be open to the few we might enjoy." Thus, Early and one-fourth of Lee's army had been dispatched on this mission. It was a bold move to break the stalemate in the trenches at Petersburg.

As the Confederates moved through Maryland, they levied ransoms on Hagerstown, $20,000; Middletown, $5,000; and finally Frederick, $200,000. Apparently, the latter figure was due to the fact that one of the Confederate officers, not very good in math, forgot to add another zero to the $20,000 figure in Hagerstown. The ransom was in money and supplies.[124]

On July 9, a small but major battle was fought on the banks of the Monocacy River, just south of Frederick. Major General Lew Wallace, commanding the Union forces, had a profound fear. He was afraid that Jubal Early would enter the front door to the White House as Lincoln departed through the back door.

Wallace fought for time and perhaps saved the Union. The weather was extremely hot, and the heat and dust added to the delay. However, by July 11, Jubal Early's army was in Silver Spring, within sight of the unfinished dome of the U.S. Capitol. However, the delay on the banks of the Monocacy had enabled Grant to send veterans from the Sixth Corps at Petersburg to bolster the defenses of Washington.

During the Confederate advance, a distinguished person went to Fort Stevens just north of Washington to observe the Confederate advance. A man was killed nearby. An officer by the name of Oliver Wendell Holmes said, "Get down you fool." The tall man was none other than President Lincoln.

Although Early was forced to retire from the gates of Washington, Confederates continued to move at will northwest of Washington. Later in the month, General John McCausland burned the city of Chambersburg in retaliation for Union acts of depredation in the South. On July 25, George Crook and his Union force were routed at Kernstown, just south of Winchester.

Enough was enough. The Confederates had to be denied access to the North from the Shenandoah Valley. Grant wrote a letter to Mr. Lincoln. It was hand-carried by his chief of staff, John Rawlings. Grant requested that the four departments in the Middle Atlantic States, West Virginia, Middle Susquehanna and Washington be consolidated and placed under one commander. This officer must have the devoted confidence of both Lincoln and Grant.

Lincoln responded with a request to meet with U.S. Grant, any time after July 28, to discuss the matter. Grant noted that he was working on a movement that might bring favorable results. This was the Battle of the Crater, which a few days later ended in a Union disaster. This occurred on July 30, the same day McCausland applied the torch to Chambersburg. Later on the same day, Grant wired Lincoln that he would meet him on July 31. Lincoln also conferred with General Montgomery Meigs, asking if the fords west of Washington could be destroyed so as to deny the Confederates access to Maryland.

Late on July 30, Lincoln embarked for another trip to Fort Monroe, accompanied by Mrs. Lincoln. The President waited at the wharf at the fort for Grant to arrive. The conference began at 10:00 a.m. on Sunday, July 31.[125]

The details of the conference are sketchy. The two discussed Early's incursion and agreed that an event of this nature must not happen again. They talked about applying pressure on all fronts against the Confederates. The Shenandoah Valley had to be cleared of all Confederate forces. The breadbasket of the Confederacy had to be destroyed. They agreed on the principle of total warfare.

The other prime consideration was the consolidation of the four departments into one department, with one commander. Lincoln inquired whether George Meade had been considered. Grant said he had talked with Meade, and he was "ready to obey orders." As always, Meade was a good soldier. There was also a discussion about naming George B. McClellan to the post. There was the possibility that McClellan would oppose Lincoln in the 1864 presidential election. Lincoln was keenly aware of the Democratic opposition to the war and of McClellan's peace advocacy. Lincoln was fighting for his political life. He was very uncertain of reelection. Placing McClellan in an important command might relieve a serious political threat. Additional Confederate victories in the Shenandoah Valley might sound the political death knell for Lincoln.[126]

The President and the general talked for five hours. They agreed on the consolidation of the departments and Union pressure on all points. Unresolved was the Union commander of the new department. Lincoln placed that matter in Grant's hands. At 5:00 p.m., the *Baltimore* departed for Washington. The vessel arrived at 5:00 a.m. on August 1.

Grant wasted no time; he was a man of action and decision. He sent a telegram to General Henry Halleck in Washington. "I want Sheridan put in command of all the troops in the field, with instructions to put himself south of the enemy and follow him to the death. Wherever the enemy goes, let our troops go also."

The brass in Washington was not happy with Grant's decision. Lincoln, Stanton and Halleck all had misgivings about the little thirty-three-year-old cavalry commander. They thought he was too young for such an important command. Grant decided to go to Washington and thence to Monocacy Junction. Reaching Monocacy, he conferred with David Hunter, the Union commander. It was obvious that Hunter did not have a grasp of the situation. Hunter saw the handwriting on the wall and asked to be relieved. Grant's response was direct and to the point, "Very well then." Hunter was directed to go to Charles Town, and a telegram was sent to Phil Sheridan.[127]

Sheridan journeyed to Washington. He went to the White House and paid his respects to the President. Lincoln wished him the best. Next was a meeting with Secretary of War Stanton. Sheridan was told that the destruction of Early's army and clearing the Shenandoah Valley was of the utmost importance to the war effort, as well as to the continuance of the Lincoln administration.

Sheridan then took the train to Monocacy Junction and met U.S. Grant at Araby, the Thomas farm. They met in an upstairs room and plotted Sheridan's strategy in the Shenandoah Valley. Early's army had to be destroyed and the Valley rendered useless for supply and maneuver. The enemy and his will to fight had to be destroyed.

Prior to Sheridan's arrival, Grant ate breakfast with the Keefer Thomas family. The general inquired as to the family loyalties. One of those present was six-year-old Virginia, one of the Thomas daughters. Grant lifted her on his lap and said, "Well, Virginia, what are your father and mother? Are they Rebels or Yankees?"

Virginia had a quick response. "Mamma, she's a Rebel, but papa, he is a Rebel when the Rebels are here and a Yankee when the Yankees are here." The little girl's answer brought a hearty laugh.

Soon, Grant departed for City Point, and Phil Sheridan went forth to assume a new command and his own Shenandoah Valley Campaign, as well as a rise to fame.

Then the military took matters into its own hands. Grant continued to tighten the noose around the Army of Northern Virginia at Petersburg. From Monocacy Junction, Phil Sheridan went forth to assume command of the Middle Military Division. During August and early September, his command grew as units from the Sixth Corps and the Nineteenth Corps, along with two divisions of George Crook's West Virginia Corps and the troopers of cavalry units commanded by Alfred T. Torbett and James H. Wilson, were assigned to his control.

By mid-September, he was ready to move. Proceeding south from Charles Town to Berryville, Sheridan then moved west and on September 19 struck Jubal Early's command east and northeast of Winchester. Sheridan's old West Point roommate, George Crook, turned the Confederate left flank, and the Confederates were routed.

Three days later, Sheridan struck the Confederate line of defense at Fisher's Hill, south of Winchester. Once again, it was Crook who turned the Confederate left flank, and the result was an overwhelming Union victory.

Things quieted down for a few weeks. The sector looked calm enough, and Sheridan left the army for a conference in Washington. While he was gone, Jubal Early's army launched a last-ditch effort to turn the tide. In the early morning hours of October 19, they struck out of the mist and fog and sent Sheridan's army reeling.

"Little Phil" arrived in Winchester in the nick of time. He galloped down the Valley Pike, rallying his retreating men and urging them to go back. The result was electrifying. This time, Sheridan's army struck back, and what had begun as a great Confederate victory ended in disaster for the Confederate cause.

Red October followed. Sheridan's men torched the Shenandoah Valley from Harpers Ferry to Staunton. Columns of heavy black smoke filled the air as barns, crops and mills were set ablaze. Sheridan stated that a crow flying over the darkened area would have trouble finding provisions. This was total warfare, destroying the will of the people to continue the struggle, torching the "breadbasket of the Confederacy" and removing the food supply.

Lincoln and Congress tendered their thanks and recognition to Philip Sheridan. He was promoted to lieutenant general. While Sheridan was destroying Early's army and the Shenandoah Valley, William T. Sherman was marching to the sea.

It was the actions of Sheridan and Sherman that turned the tide in the autumn of 1864, and it was the vote of the soldiers that continued the Lincoln presidency and thwarted the efforts of the former soldier George B. McClellan.

TRAVELS IN 1865

Hampton Roads

In early February, President Lincoln traveled on the USS *Bat* to Hampton Roads to meet with Confederate leaders in an effort to end the war. However, the negotiations were fruitless, and Lincoln reported failure to his cabinet on February 4. The South held on to states' rights and pride.[128]

On the night of February 22, Washington, D.C., was gaily illuminated. As the nation celebrated the birthday of the father of our country, citizens realized that the war could not last much longer. The flag of the Union flew over Fort Fisher, Columbia, Charleston and Savannah. Grant had Lee bottled up in the trenches around Petersburg, and William T. Sherman was pressing on.

On the morning of March 4, there was a parade on Pennsylvania Avenue. A light drizzle fell. It was cold and gusty. Then it was time for Mr. Lincoln to be sworn in for his second term. However, he and others had to endure the swearing in of Vice President Andrew Johnson, who was almost incoherent. Johnson had been ill—some thought he was drunk.

Included in Lincoln's Second Inaugural address were these famous words:

> *With malice toward none, with charity for all…to do all which may achieve a just and lasting peace, among ourselves and with all nations.*[129]

Just like the Gettysburg Address, there was a mixed reaction. Some had very negative comments, while others thought it was like a plea for peace, a benediction and a deep cry for unification.

That night, nearly six thousand persons descended on the White House to meet and greet the chief executive. Lincoln shook hands with them all. An aide felt that Lincoln did not seem like himself.[130]

The presidency takes its toll, physically and mentally, on every chief executive. Mr. Lincoln was no exception. The photographs from 1861 compared to 1865 show a remarkable difference. By the spring of 1865, many were commenting on how burdened and careworn Mr. Lincoln looked.

By this time, Robert, over the objections of his mother, had entered the army. However, he had a relatively safe position on the staff of U.S. Grant. One day, Julia Grant asked Robert why his father and mother did not come to City Point for a visit. Captain Robert replied that he supposed they would if they did not think they were imposing. General Grant was present during the conversation. He was fond of the President, feeling that Mr. Lincoln understood him and never questioned him about his operations. Walking to the telegraph office, he sent a communiqué.[131]

Donald C. Pfanz, the author of *Abraham Lincoln at City Point*, noted that Lincoln's ready acceptance of Grant's invitation is not hard to understand. Since the Second Inaugural, the President had been working night and day and was constantly being sought by mothers seeking some benefit for their sons in the military. A trip to City Point would provide an escape from Washington and a much-needed respite. The presence of the chief executive might also motivate the troops for the upcoming campaign.[132]

Originally, the President had considered traveling alone. After receiving General Grant's invitation, he summoned Secretary of the Navy Gustavus V. Fox to his office and informed him of his plans. Fox selected the USS *Bat* for transportation. A little later, Fox brought the commander of the *Bat*, John Barnes, to the White House. Barnes remarked about the sparse accommodations. Lincoln brushed them aside. The next day, Barnes returned, and Lincoln apologetically said that Mrs. Lincoln was also going to be traveling to City Point. Mrs. Lincoln wanted to see Robert and informed Barnes of that fact. Thus, a switch was made to the *River Queen*, with the *Bat* following as escort. The navy had major concerns about the safety of the President.[133]

Nevertheless, on March 23, Mrs. Lincoln's personal maid, as well as William Crook, the President's bodyguard, were also on board, as was Captain Charles Penrose, selected by Secretary Stanton to look out for the President. And, of course, son Tad was along for the great adventure.

Crook had little time to pack his belongings and rush to the Seventh Street Wharf. From there the *River Queen* and the *Bat* departed at 1:00 p.m. A cold front from the North descended with strong winds. However, Mr. Lincoln remained on deck until the ship cleared Alexandria. The President sat with Captain Bradford and listened to the veteran officer's tales of fighting pirates and running the blockade. Earlier, he had given Crook and Tad a tour of the ship. The President and his wife shared one room, while Crook and Tad shared another. The storm had made the waters of the Potomac and the Chesapeake rather rough. Soon Crook was seasick, as was Mr. Lincoln. As on previous occasions, the President attributed his upset stomach to bad water. Thus, the *River Queen* pulled into Fort Monroe for fresh water.[134]

The James River was more tranquil. The *River Queen* departed Fort Monroe and reached City Point at about 8:30 p.m. Lights shone from the boats moored at the docks and from the tented cities of the military. When the ship docked around 9:00 p.m., General Grant and several staff officers were present to meet Lincoln. The President escorted the general and his wife up the gangplank and on board the *River Queen*. He and the general entered one room to confer, while Mrs. Lincoln and Mrs. Grant went to another room.

The President and General Grant had a very congenial discussion. Grant briefed the President on the state of military affairs and his expectations. As the two powerful men and their wives concluded the evening, it was agreed that they would meet in the morning and proceed to review the troops.

When March 23, 1865, dawned, President Lincoln had but three weeks remaining in his life. Two of those three weeks were spent at City Point with General Grant and visiting Petersburg and Richmond. We'll look briefly at the two-week timeframe and then at the two weeks in detail.

The President, Mrs. Lincoln and Tad departed from the Seventh Street Wharf on the *River Queen* on March 23. A review scheduled for the twenty-fifth was canceled when the Confederates attacked Fort Stedman. Lincoln went to the front to see the action. On the twenty-sixth, Mr. Lincoln was taken to see the Malvern Hill battlefield and review the troops commanded by General Ord. Mrs. Lincoln flew into a rage because Mrs. Ord rode near the President. The twenty-seventh took Lincoln to Point of Rocks. He also walked into the woods to see the tree where Pocahontas supposedly saved the life of Captain John Smith. During the trip, Lincoln amazed the soldiers by chopping wood and holding an axe at arm's length longer than any of the troops. That night, he met on board the *River Queen* with Generals Grant and Sherman and Admiral Porter, discussing Confederate surrender terms.

City Point, 1865. *Library of Congress.*

On April 1, Mary sailed for Washington, leaving Tad with the President. During the night, Lincoln had his bad dream about being assassinated.

Lee evacuated Richmond on April 2. On the third and fourth, Lincoln and Tad visited Petersburg and Richmond. Mrs. Lincoln and some government officials returned on April 6. Lincoln returned to Petersburg on April 7, spending the day visiting Union wounded.

SATURDAY, MARCH 25

According to Donald Pfanz, the morning dawned cool and damp. Fog hung over the areas. Once the sun rose and the mists burned off, a warm day was promised.[135]

Things were astir early. There was the sound of battle in the area. Around 6:00 a.m., the Confederates had tried to break out of the lines of encirclement at Fort Stedman. Grant was prepared. He had been expecting a move of the enemy, who was becoming desperate. He immediately sent a telegram to General Edward O.C. Ord to "be ready to take advantage of the situation." The President felt better and had breakfast with Captain Barnes, Captain Penrose and Tad. As he finished, Captain Robert Lincoln arrived. The young officer reported that the battle was still in progress but that the enemy had been repulsed. The President gave his son a message to be sent to Secretary Stanton describing "a little rumpus up at the time… ending where it began." This attack, though, was the beginning of the end for Robert E. Lee and the Army of Northern Virginia.[136]

A little later, Admiral David Porter arrived to pay his respects. The admiral and the President walked to Grant's headquarters on a bluff. The President requested a trip to the front. Grant initially denied the request, but upon learning that it was safe, he acquiesced.

Around noon, a special train was made up, and a large group traveled to the headquarters of General George G. Meade. Mr. Lincoln mounted a horse and rode over the battlefield. He saw some of those killed in action being buried. When it was time to leave, additional cars were added to the train to take the wounded back to City Point. Upon the return to City Point, Lincoln was fatigued, physically and emotionally drained. Thus, he declined an invitation to have supper with General Grant and returned to the *River Queen*. Earlier in the day, he had telegraphed Secretary Stanton, noting his safe arrival and stating that he was just five miles from the front.

During the tour of the battlefield, Lincoln rode one of Grant's horses, Jeff Davis. However, the horse was a little small for the tall, lanky man from Illinois. On future trips, Grant rode Jeff Davis while the President rode Cincinnati.[137]

SUNDAY, MARCH 26

The President and Captain Barnes ate breakfast together. The President spoke wistfully of the suffering of the soldiers and civilians and expressed the hope that the terrible war would soon be over. Then there was a walk to Grant's headquarters. Admiral Porter, George G. Meade, Edward Ord and Phil Sheridan were present. Lincoln in his humor said he expected a cavalryman to be large, six-foot-four. However, looking at little Phil and knowing of his exploits, he said, "I guess five feet four will do in a pinch." Sheridan had come from the Shenandoah Valley to add further punishment to the Army of Northern Virginia.[138]

Lincoln then turned his attention to three small, purring kittens. The mother had died. Lincoln, touched by their plight, addressed Colonel Bowers, saying, "I hope you will take care of these poor creatures…and see that they are given plenty of milk."[139] This act was another example of his kindness, simplicity and compassion.

At 11:00 a.m., Mr. Lincoln, along with his wife, General and Mrs. Grant, Sheridan and Ord boarded the *Mary Martin*. The President was in a somber and reflective mood.

When the *Mary Martin* reached Deep Bottom, those on board were greeted with cheers from hundreds of Sheridan's men bathing and washing their clothes. Near Trent's Reach was Porter's naval fluvial. The sailors also cheered as the *Mary Martin* approached. Lincoln and the guests on the *Mary Martin* had a sumptuous lunch on Admiral Porter's flagship.

The Presidential party went ashore and rode over muddy roads to a parade to witness a review of black troops under the command of Godfrey Weitzel. The President rode on Cincinnati. Mrs. Lincoln was riding in an ambulance with Julia Grant. Mrs. Ord was supposed to be in the ambulance, but it was full so she mounted a horse. Mary Ord was a nice-looking lady and very good at handling a horse.

Short of temper and with a jealous personality, Mary Lincoln became infuriated at the sight of Mrs. Ord riding in the company of the President. "How dare she? Who does she think she is? I'm the wife of the President. What does she mean flirting with my husband?" It was the Sabbath, but there were domestic fireworks. Mary Lincoln's anger mounted. Her tirade was heard by many. At one time, it was thought she would jump from the ambulance. Mrs. Grant tried to calm her down and restrain her. Then Mrs. Lincoln turned on Julia, accusing her of wanting to assume the White House.[140]

Meanwhile, the President was riding toward the review, unaware of Mary's histrionics. John Barnes noted that the President had on a long-frocked coat, black vest and rumpled shirt. He also wore a high silk hat; occasionally, as Cincinnati jogged along, his white socks could be seen.

The Presidential party rode along the lines of massed troops. They came to "present arms." Meanwhile, the bands played martial and patriotic music. Little Jesse Grant was in the party, so proud and so impressed with his father.

"Beside Mr. Lincoln, father looked small." The sight of the President gave Jesse a feeling of awe that lasted a lifetime.[141]

The ambulance with Mrs. Lincoln and Mrs. Grant arrived while the review was still in progress. Once again Mary Lincoln flew into a rage. There was that woman again, riding near the President. The situation was even worse, as Mary Ord was riding beside the President. Mrs. Ord spotted the ambulance and galloped across the field to meet the other ladies—unaware of the firestorm into which she rode. Mary Lincoln called her every name in the book, hurling accusations and insults for all to hear. Mrs. Ord broke down in tears and had to be assisted from the area. Lincoln did not learn all the details until later.

Then it was back to the *Mary Martin* and the return trip to City Point. Returning to the *River Queen*, Lincoln brought a military band on board. He had hoped for a nice evening. However, Mary was still fuming and berated General Ord in the presence of the guests for the behavior of his wife. She even urged that General Ord be removed from command. Mr. Lincoln was mortified.

Mary Lincoln was not one to forgive and forget. Later that night, Captain Barnes was called to the Presidential quarters. It was evident that the Lincolns had been quarreling. Mary wanted Barnes's account of the event but remained unforgiving.[142]

Monday, March 27

The day began with breakfast aboard the *River Queen*. The President and Tad spent some time together. The President then went to the stateroom to take care of some office matters. Captain Barnes came aboard. Lincoln was very kind to him, as he had always admired him, and he was still reeling from the nasty manner in which Mary had treated the naval officer. Lincoln read the reports of the action at Fort Stedman as well as casualty reports.[143]

Barnes and Mr. Lincoln walked through the busy supply depot. Stores of all kind were piled up, ready for transportation to the front. There was hay and oats for the horses and mules as well. Lincoln and his companion climbed the bluff to army headquarters. Excitement was in the air. There was a feeling that the end was in sight.

Lincoln's spirits were buoyed by the feeling and the activity. He engaged in telling some stories from days gone by. He was a master at the art and craft of telling stories. They were never told just for the sake of telling them, but rather to illustrate a fact or point. At noon, the President returned to the *River Queen* for another trip on the Appomattox River to Point of Rocks. This was his third trip. General and Mrs. Grant shared the journey, as did Admiral Porter, Captain Barnes and son Robert.[144]

Point of Rocks is now a Virginia State Park. It is four miles west of City Point. The Presidential party had lunch by the Appomattox River. Grant and Lincoln strolled through the woods to see the spot where Pocahontas supposedly saved the life of Captain John Smith. Lincoln and Grant climbed a tower to observe the tents of the Confederate troops several miles away. In the evening, Mr. Lincoln shared with Sherman and Grant that he wanted generous peace terms; although the South had been the enemy, he wanted no harsh peace—"Let them up easy." Sherman was impressed, saying, "Of all the men I ever met, he seems to possess more of the elements of greatness, combined with goodness than any other." It was anticipated that Petersburg and Richmond would soon fall, causing the collapse of the Confederacy.[145]

Mrs. Lincoln was still pouting. Captain Barnes had had a rough trip; he was on Mary's list of enemies. He had failed to support her attack on Mrs. Ord. When he offered her a chair, at the suggestion of Mrs. Grant, Mrs. Lincoln refused it. In fact, she asked Mrs. Grant to tell Barnes that she objected to his presence. Thus, at the first stop, he departed.[146]

Tuesday, March 28

This morning, General Grant hosted a reception for General William T. Sherman at his City Point headquarters. Dr. Pfanz felt that this might have been the greatest gathering of military brass at one site at one time during the war. George Meade, Edward Ord, Phil Sheridan and Rufus Ingalls (the quartermaster general of the army) were present, as was Admiral Porter and possibly generals from the western armies.[147]

After a while, Grant and Porter left the reception to confer with the President aboard the *River Queen*, which was anchored in the James River. A small tug carried them to the President's vessel. Grant and Sherman wanted to pay their respects to Mrs. Lincoln. However, she declined to see them. She said she was not feeling well and wished to be excused.

General U.S. Grant with his wife and his son, Jesse, at City Point. *Library of Congress*.

Those meeting on the *River Queen* held the destiny of the nation in their hands. Grant began the discussion by giving an overview of the military situation. Sheridan's cavalry was in the process of cutting the railroad supply lines into Petersburg. If successful, the fate of Lee and his army would be sealed. It was thought that Lee could not escape and link up with Johnston in North Carolina. Sherman felt he could more than handle the combined forces should that occur. Lee would be faced with starvation or the necessity of seeking to break out.

Twice during the conference, Mr. Lincoln expressed concern about Sherman's absence from his command. Sherman reassured the President that the army was in good hands, as General Schofield was "a very capable commander."[148]

Sherman noticed the physical and emotional appearance of Mr. Lincoln, saying that he seemed almost lifeless, looking "so careworn and haggard." Sherman asked the chief executive if he was ready for the postwar haggling and Congressional fighting. There were those who wanted the South to be treated very harshly, almost as traitors. There were some moderates and then others who desired reconciliation as quickly as possible. Lincoln desired the Confederate soldiers to be pardoned and to return home as quickly as possible. Mr. Lincoln authorized General Sherman to reassure Governor Vance of North Carolina that they would be recognized as citizens once they laid down their arms. The Presidential peace terms were forgiving, generous and compassionate, "aimed to bind up the wounds of the country."

Lincoln was concerned about further bloodshed. He hated the thought of continued warfare and asked, "Must another battle be fought?" Sherman bluntly replied that the answer rested with the Confederates' decision. They could continue to fight or lay down their arms. Lincoln once again advocated liberal terms to the defeated Southerners. "Let them go….They could use their horses to plow their fields and their guns to shoot crows….Give them the most liberal and honorable terms."[149]

Sherman informed the President that his men had destroyed the railroads in North Carolina. There was no way they could be rebuilt. He had Johnston in his grip and felt that in two weeks the end would come. Lincoln urged Sherman to give Johnston the same liberal terms he hoped Grant would give to Lee. "Let there be no further bloodshed."[150]

Wednesday, March 29

Dawn brought bustling activity at City Point. The final campaign was ready to begin—the battle to end the war was at hand. Trains were headed west, carrying rations and ammunition for ten days of activity, as well as food for the animals. There were also new mounts for the cavalry. Sheridan, George G. Meade and Edward Ord were at the front, and Grant was preparing to go. "The curtain was rising on the last act" of the war in Virginia.[151]

Mr. Lincoln came ashore at about 8:30 a.m. He chatted with General Grant at his headquarters as he prepared to move toward the front. An hour later, General Grant kissed his beloved Julia goodbye. Colonel Porter, like Sherman, noted the deep furrows on Lincoln's face and the huge dark circles under his eyes. Lincoln also bade a touching farewell to Captain Robert Lincoln, telling him to do his duty. General John Rawlins, Grant's chief of staff, grasped Lincoln's hand firmly and said, "I hope we shall have better luck than we have had."[152]

Lincoln replied that the army's luck "is my luck and the country's." Then his voice trailed off. He seemed lost in thought, "except [for] the poor fellows who are killed." The train began to pull away. The officers raised their hats in respect to the President. Waving his hand, he said, "Goodbye Gentlemen. God Bless you all."[153]

In midmorning, there was the heavy sound of thunder. It was cannon fire from the front. Being interested in military matters, he telegraphed General Grant asking from what direction was the enemy attack. Next came a dispatch to General Griffin: "How do things look now?" And still later, to General Grant: "What if anything have you observed on your front today?" The cannonade began after Grant, Meade, Ord and Sheridan had departed for the front and General Sherman departed for North Carolina. In the afternoon, Lincoln rode with Admiral Porter on a tug that Lincoln called "my old buggy." That night, a cold, steady rain fell on City Point and the battle lines to the west.[154]

FRIDAY, MARCH 31

This was a rather quiet day at City Point. Secretary Seward arrived from Washington to confer with the President. The rain continued to fall, creating a sea of mud. The President spent the bulk of the day, as well as the next several days, at the cabin of Colonel Bowers. He often spoke with Samuel Beckwith, who operated the telegraph in the adjoining room. He began to consider whether he should return to Washington. Stanton thought that the end was near and that the President should stay to see the end. Lincoln also conversed with Governor Andrew Curtin and General Carl S. Schurz, who were there.

Lincoln was in a melancholy mood. Throughout the war, he was always saddened when Thursday came. This was the day when battlefield losses were posted at the War Department. Lincoln often went to see the lists and became morose at the numbers. Now he was aware that Grant was preparing a large-scale attack and that there would be additional loss of life. Grant sent a telegram stating that the Confederates had been driven back several miles and that four battle flags had been captured.

Mr. Lincoln read the dispatches from the front as the rain began to fall. It was a gloomy night. Then, at 10:15 p.m., there was more noise, fighting around Petersburg. Mr. Lincoln fell asleep to the sound of the rain falling and the cannons booming in the distance.

SATURDAY, APRIL 1

Time was running out for Mr. Lincoln and the Confederacy. Mary Lincoln departed for Washington. She had spent the better part of five days in seclusion on the *River Queen*. Stress and her personality had caused a lot of trouble and embarrassment for the President. The First Lady departed on the USS *Monohassett*. Tad and the President had walked her to the dock.[155]

As Mrs. Lincoln headed for Washington, cannon fire could already be heard from the front. Lincoln made his way to the cabin of Colonel Bowers to await communiqués from the front. G.K. Warren's Fifth Corps and Sheridan's cavalry had attacked Confederate lines west of Petersburg.

Forgetting that he had not arranged for Mary's transportation from the Navy Yard to the White House, Lincoln wired Secretary Stanton requesting a coach for Mary. He also sent one to Alfonson Dunn, the White House coachman.

The day passed very slowly. Toward evening, dispatches began to arrive. Sheridan's men were attacking the enemy at a very important crossroads known as Five Forks. Rebel lines had been broken, and many flags and prisoners had been captured. From the *River Queen*, Lincoln could hear the sound of cannons and see the flashes of artillery. Would the attacks bring an end to the conflict?[156]

The President laid down to sleep. But it was a long time coming, and then there was a terrible dream. Lincoln later said:

> *About ten days ago, I retired very late. I had been up waiting for important dispatches from the front. I could not have been long in bed when I fell into a slumber, for I was weary. I soon began to dream. There seemed to be a death-like stillness about me. Then I heard subdued sobs, as if a number of people were weeping. I thought I left my bed and wandered downstairs.*
>
> *There the silence was broken by the same pitiful sobbing, but the mourners were invisible. I went from room to room; no living person was in sight, but the same mournful sounds of distress met me as I passed along. It was light in all the rooms; every object was familiar to me; but where were all the people who were grieving as if their hearts would break? I was puzzled and alarmed. What could be the meaning of all this? Determined to find the cause of a state of things so mysterious and so shocking, I kept on until I arrived at the East Room, which I entered. There I met with a sickening surprise. Before me was a catafalque, on which rested a corpse wrapped in funeral vestments. Around it were stationed soldiers who were acting as guards; and there was a throng of people, some gazing mournfully upon the corpse, whose face was covered, others weeping pitifully. "Who is dead in the White House?" I demanded of one of the soldiers. "The President," was his answer; "he was killed by an assassin!" Then came a*

General Edward Ord and his family. *Library of Congress.*

loud burst of grief from the crowd, which awoke me from my dream. I slept no more that night; and although it was only a dream, I have been strangely annoyed by it ever since.[157]

Unable to sleep, the troubled President got dressed and walked outside. In the east, the sky was beginning to gray. Another day would soon be at hand—would it bring victory or defeat?[158]

Sunday, April 2

Saturday, April 1, had been a disaster for the Army of Northern Virginia. Phil Sheridan had broken their lines at the important road Junction at Five Forks. Early on the Sabbath, R.E. Lee sent a telegram to the War Department in Richmond indicating that he could no longer hold the lines at Petersburg. The Confederate War Department was located just four doors from St. Paul's Episcopal Church.[159]

By the time the telegram arrived, Jefferson Davis was at church for Sunday morning worship. The courier walked to the church and gave the communiqué to the sexton, William Irving. Mr. Irving walked up the center aisle to pew 63, tapped President Jefferson Davis on the shoulder and gave him the message. President Davis read the message and departed immediately.

City and CSA officials realized that Richmond was doomed. Plans were made for the immediate evacuation. Important papers were piled in Capital Square and set afire. The news spread like wildfire. Soon there was chaos. People of all ages sought to escape the city.

At 8:00 p.m., Jefferson Davis and the remnants of the Confederate government departed the Danville Station. Richard Ewell, acting under orders from Secretary of War John Breckinridge, began destroying the Confederate stores, including whiskey. The potent alcohol ran in the gutters. Anxious and troubled civilians tried to save as much of it as possible. Order and discipline vanished. Soon drunken masses began plundering whatever was left.

Later in the evening, Richard Ewell gave the order the torch the Shockhoe Warehouse containing huge quantities of cotton and tobacco. There was a gentle breeze blowing. Sparks were quickly carried into the downtown area of Richmond. Soon the capital of the Confederacy was ablaze. Before dawn, more than nine hundred buildings had gone up in smoke. Every bank was gone, as well as the primary business establishments.[160]

Lincoln was comforted by a telegram from Mary that she had arrived safely in Washington.[161] President Lincoln was on the *Malvern*, as the *River Queen* had taken Mrs. Lincoln to Washington. Admiral Porter offered Mr. Lincoln his quarters. However, he refused and took a smaller room. Later, Lincoln said that the two nights aboard the *Malvern* were among the best he had experienced. He was away from everything and everybody, and he liked Admiral Porter.[162]

He put his shoes and socks outside the room's door—there were holes in his socks. At 9:30 p.m., there was a huge explosion. Lincoln leaped up, fearing that a Union ship had exploded. However, it was the beginning of the explosions that rocked Richmond. It was the beginning of the end for the Confederacy.

MONDAY, APRIL 3

Murky smoke arose from downtown Richmond, and in some parts of the city, the fire continued to burn. At about 3:00 a.m. Mayor Joseph Mayo, eighty years of age, and several other officials began driving eastward in two horse-drawn rigs on the New Market Road. Soon they met a detachment of Union soldiers, the Fourth Massachusetts Cavalry, under Major A.H. Stephens and Major E.E. Graves. The detachment was small, just forty men. Mayor Mayo had a note for the commander of the Union forces in front of Richmond, requesting that Union troops take over the city and maintain order. The note was delivered to General Weitzel. The general followed the cavalry detachment into Richmond and at 8:15 a.m. accepted the surrender in front of city hall. The Union commander dispatched some of his troops to help fight the remaining fires and smoldering embers.[163]

Lieutenant Johnston Livingston DePeyster, a member of Weitzel's staff, climbed to the roof of the capitol building and hoisted the "Stars and Stripes" and the regimental flag. Meanwhile, the regimental band played "The Star-Spangled Banner."

Lincoln awoke to the news that Petersburg had fallen. He immediately sent a note to Mary, as well as to Secretary Stanton. The President then had breakfast with Admiral Porter. They were joined by Captain Barnes, who had returned from a trip to North Carolina. Lincoln inquired as to the situation there. Lincoln then announced his desire to visit Petersburg, inviting the naval officers to accompany him. The three of them walked to the railroad depot and took a special train to the front. Lincoln read a newspaper en route. Tad and William Crook were also on board. The original destination was the Patrick Street Station. However, a message was received from Robert Lincoln saying that he would meet his father at the Hancock Station farther east. The train slowed at one point to allow a large number of captured Confederates to cross the tracks. Lincoln muttered, "Poor boys. Poor boys."[164]

At the Hancock Station, the President was met by Robert and a detachment of the Fifth U.S. Cavalry. Mr. Lincoln mounted Cincinnati and began to ride. Poor Admiral Porter was on a horse that stumbled a lot. Lincoln, who was in good spirits, noted, "Admiral, you missed your profession. You should have been a circus rider."

In Petersburg, the party stopped at Fort Mahone, a key position in the Confederate line. There were bloated bodies lying around. Mr. Lincoln shed a tear, and his countenance became very sad.[165]

Petersburg had held out for a long time. Now the "Stars and Stripes" fluttered over the city. Mr. Lincoln and the group rode to 21 Market Street, where Grant had established temporary headquarters. Grant was seated on the porch. The two met and greeted each other warmly. Horace Porter said he had never seen the President look happier. He believed that the President wanted to hug Grant rather than merely shake hands. Grant discussed his plans, and Lincoln revealed his anxiety about the final campaigns in Virginia and North Carolina.

Grant and Lincoln then talked of the consequences of the defeat of the Confederate armies, as well as the steps to peace and reconstruction. Lincoln again spoke of leniency and compassion.

Meanwhile, Tad was getting restless. He was a growing boy and was getting hungry. A Union officer realized the situation and gave Tad a sandwich. Tad gulped it down, replying that he had indeed been very hungry. The sandwich was just what he needed.[166]

During the visit, the owner of the house appeared. Lincoln, who had a good memory, recognized him as a member of the Whig Party and a friend from Lincoln's Congressional days. Wallace invited the group inside. However, the men declined, and Mr. Wallace brought the President a high-backed chair.

Before leaving Petersburg, Lincoln paid a visit to the home of Confederate general Roger Pryor. The two had also served in Congress together.

Knocking at the door, he was met by Mrs. Pryor. She said that General Lee was still in the field fighting and that her husband was a paroled prisoner.

She refused to let the President in. However, on a more cordial note, a little girl approached the President and gave him some flowers and a smile.[167]

Walking through the town, Mr. Lincoln saw the devastation. African Americans turned out to praise the tall man from Illinois, while the white populace remained indoors. There was the pungent smell of tobacco sheaves and bales lying everywhere. Some in the Presidential party grabbed the three-pound bales. Tad also obtained some—not to smoke, but because everybody else was doing it.

April 3 was indeed a day of good news. There was the triumphal visit to Petersburg, and when Lincoln returned to City Point, there was great news:

> *We Took Richmond at 8:15 This Morning. I Captured Many Guns. The Enemy Left in Great Haste. The City Is on Fire in One Place, Am Making Every Effort to Put It Out. The People Received Us with Enthusiastic Expressions of Joy.*

> *To Secretary of War Stanton from General Weitzel,*
> *transmitted from City Point, Virginia at 11 a.m., April 3, 1865*

Lincoln read the dispatch and then shared the joy with everybody else. The President's face was aglow. The burdens of war seemed to lift. It was almost as though he was transformed. There was light at the end of the tunnel. However, on the negative side, there was a telegram from Secretary Stanton congratulating the President on the victory but warning him of the danger of visiting Richmond. Lincoln told his cabinet member not to worry:

> *Hon. Sec. of War Washington, D.C.*

> *Yours received. Thanks for your caution; but I have already been to Petersburg, staid [sic] with Gen. Grant an hour & a half and returned here. It is certain now that Richmond is in our hands, and I think I will go there tomorrow. I will take care of myself.*

Mr. Lincoln then began walking to the *Malvern* but stopped to share the good news with Julia Grant. The *Malvern* was tied up to a prisoner of war ship. Once again the President saw the lean, haggard Confederates, and his countenance turned to sadness.[168]

TUESDAY, APRIL 4

At 8:00 a.m., Mr. Lincoln ordered Samuel A. Beckwith, the cipher operator at Grant's headquarters, to accompany him to Richmond. Three vessels began the trip: the *River Queen*, the *Bat* and the *Malvern*. Lincoln and Tad began the journey on the *River Queen*. For Lincoln, it was a crowning moment. His presidency had been devoted to preserving and restoring the fractured Union. The President said, "Thank God I have lived to see this. It seems to me that I have been dreaming a horrid dream for four years, and now the nightmare is gone. I want to see Richmond."[169]

The *Bat* and *River Queen* experienced navigational problems from two sources: sandbars and the Confederate mines that still peppered the James River. Likewise, there were some scuttled CSA ships in the river. Lincoln therefore transferred to the *Malvern*. When it could proceed no farther, the Presidential party transferred to a naval barge. The sailors rowed the President to Rocketts Landing. Landing with Mr. Lincoln was Admiral Porter, Captain Penrose, Tad and W.H. Crook. Rocketts was about one hundred yards from Libby Prison.[170]

It was 11:00 a.m. at Thirty-First and Main Street. The President walked hand in hand with Tad. There was a twelve-man guard with fixed bayonets. Smoke still hung over the city, and the smell of burning embers was ever-present.

On Clay Street, Colonel Thomas T. Graves, an aide to General Weitzel, saw a crowd coming, "headed by President Lincoln, who was walking with his long, careless stride, and looking about with an interested air and taking in everything." Mr. Lincoln wanted to know how far it was to President Davis's house. Colonel Graves escorted him to the home, which had been vacated on Sunday night. A glass of cold water revived the tired President.

Upon arrival, he was ushered into the reception room, and a housekeeper remarked that it had been President Davis's office. Mr. Lincoln seated himself and remarked, "This must have been President Davis's chair." He crossed his legs and had a faraway look. A few moments later, he inquired of Colonel Graves if the housekeeper were still present. Upon learning that she had left, he jumped up and said with a boyish manner, "Come, let's look at the house." The President and Colonel Graves then took a rather complete tour. As the group descended the staircase, General Weitzel entered. Immediately, the boyish expression left the President's face, and he took upon himself a serious look. Duty must be resumed.[171]

Soon Judge John A. Campbell, Confederate general Anderson and some others arrived and asked for an audience with Mr. Lincoln. This was granted. The meeting was held behind closed doors.

Judge Campbell realized that Mr. Lincoln expected some type of formal message from the Confederate government. Campbell said that he had none to give. Campbell also informed the President that he had conferred with Secretary of War John C. Breckinridge, the former vice president of the United States, saying that he would remain in Richmond, hoping to see Mr. Lincoln and discuss peace. Campbell said that he had no authority to do anything, but "the war is over, and all that remains to be done is to compose the country."[172]

General Weitzel summarized the closed door talks by saying, "Mr. Lincoln insisted that he could not talk with any rebels until they had laid down their arms and surrendered." Then he would go as far as possible to prevent "the shedding of another drop of blood." Lincoln reassured Campbell that the people of the North were tired of war and wanted it to end as quickly as possible.

Mr. Campbell and the other gentlemen reassured Mr. Lincoln that if he would allow the Virginia legislature to meet, it would at once repeal the ordinance of secession and then General Robert E. Lee and every other Virginian would submit—this would amount to the virtual destruction of the Army of Northern Virginia and eventually the surrender of all the other Rebel armies. It would ensure perfect peace in the shortest possible time.[173] Mr. Lincoln had lunch with General Weitzel. They then mounted a carriage and rode through the crowded streets of Richmond. Weitzel described Lincoln's reception as "enthusiastic in the extreme." Colonel Graves was the official escort for the President and the general. Additional security was provided by a troop of black cavalry. There was a brief stop at the capitol. Then Graves took them to Libby Prison and Castle Thunder. During the ride, General Weitzel inquired of the President as to the treatment of the captives and the fallen commonwealth of Virginia. Mr. Lincoln remarked that he did not wish to give any orders on the subject but, as he expressed it, "If I were in your place, I'd let 'em up easy, let 'em up easy."[174]

One of the stories concerning the Presidential visit to Richmond involved George Pickett. According to some sources, Mr. Lincoln went to the door of a Richmond house. Upon answering the knock, the lady of the house beheld "a tall, gaunt, sad faced man in ill-fitting clothes standing outside." The man said, "I am Abraham Lincoln." The woman gasped, "The President." The tall, lean figure said, "No, Abraham Lincoln, George's old friend." They had known each other prior to the war.

Mrs. Pickett was holding her ten-month-old son in her arms. Lincoln took the lad in his arms and gave him a kiss. He had been so close to his own boys, especially Tad. As the President returned the little Pickett boy to his mother, he said, "Tell your father, that I forgive him for the sake of your bright eyes."

Charles C. Coffin, a Boston correspondent, was nearby. He saw Mr. Lincoln walking up a hill and said to a black man, "Would you like to see the man who gave you your freedom—Abraham Lincoln?":

> *"Is that Massa Lincoln, sure enough?" "That is he." The man rushed forward toward Mr. Lincoln shouting, "Bless the Lord! The Great Messiah! I knowed him as soon as I seen him…come to free his children from bondage. Glory Hallelujah!" The old man fell on his knees and tried to kiss Lincoln's feet.*[175]

The President was ill at ease handing this adulation. "Don't kneel to me…. You must kneel to God only, and thank him for [your] liberty…but you may rest assured that so long as I live no one shall put a shackle on your limbs."

Such joy Charles Coffin had never witnessed. Six sailors wearing their round blue caps, short jackets and sagging pants, carrying carbines, were the advance guard. Admiral Porter and W.H. Crook walked on one side of the President, while Tad walked on the other.

The crowd became a surging mass of men, women and children. Soldiers saw him and cheered. The President was the tallest person in the group, so he was easily spotted.

A black lady was standing in a doorway when the President passed. She shouted, "Thank you, dear Jesus, for this, thank you, Jesus!" A friend standing by her side clapped her hands and shouted, "Bless de Lord." Another lady threw her bonnet in the air and shouted, "God bless you, Mass Linkum."

Some of the white residents peered from the corner of their windows. Some turned away. And one lady wrote of the President, "He seemed tired and old—and I must say, with due respect to the President of the United States, I thought him to be the ugliest man I ever seen."

Phil Sheridan was pressing the Confederate army, close on its heels, nipping almost like a hound at its cornered prey. The race was for the vital railroad junction at Burkeville, fifteen miles southwest of Amelia. If Lee could reach Burkeville, he might be able to escape and link up with Joe Johnston's forces in North Carolina. Sheridan therefore ordered his former West Point roommate, George Crook, to strike for the railroad station at Jetersville, midway between Amelia and Burkeville. The objective was to get ahead of Lee and block his escape route. The Union army had a shorter path—twenty miles, in fact. Grant seemed to have all the advantages: more troops, an abundance of food and ammunition. The Confederates were running for their lives and survival. Yet many in the ranks of the Army of Northern Virginia were hopeful. They were out of the trenches. If they could find food at Amelia, they believed they could still whip the Yankees in a pitched battle. However, they were fighting not only the Yankees but also hunger and exhaustion, as well as a lack of all vital military supplies.

Prior to the fall of Richmond, Lee had ordered meat, bread and other rations sent to Amelia or Danville. Imagine his surprise when he reached Amelia and not a single ration was to be found. Confederate soldiers were all around Amelia, hungry and without food. There was anger over who to blame about the lack of food. Lee begged the residents for the sake of his men and horses. They had nothing to share. And by late afternoon on April 4, Crook's cavalry and Griffin's Fifth Corps had reached Jetersville. Sheridan was between Lee and the main rail depot.

Sheridan felt that he could bag the Confederate army and wanted to attack. This required Grant's orders. The supreme commander made a four-hour ride through the Virginia countryside with just a small escort. The decision was that it was too late to launch a major attack.

The President demanded only three things:

Peace, Union, and Abolition.

Any and all items apart from these three central issues were open to consideration and negotiation. But a new item had been added, and it had to do with confiscation. Essentially, the President was offering the Confederacy a choice of forgiveness or retribution. Federal armies had already seized a lot of property in the South. The states that gave up the struggle an embraced the Union would have property restored; those who fought on would not—it was as simple as that. Proceeds from confiscated objects would help defray the Union cost of the war.

Lincoln then spoke about amnesty. He said he could not offer blanket amnesty but would offer pardons "on an individual basis to anyone who requested it." He promised to "save any repentant sinner from hanging." Jefferson Davis was exempt from pardon; he would have to stand trial. In a concession to the Virginians, Lincoln waived a provision requiring the citizens to take an oath of allegiance to the government of the United States.

Judge Campbell then spoke, urging the President to suspend hostilities and open peace negotiations with the Confederate government. Previously, there had been a division of thought on this issue between the Southern government and military. Now Richmond and Petersburg had fallen. Davis had little political power, and the armies of the Confederacy were dwindling. In fact, the Confederacy was ready to collapse. However, they wanted to surrender with honor and dignity. Campbell handed the President some plans he had devised.

Lincoln announced his plan to convene the Virginia legislature for the purpose of restoring Virginia to the Union. The President compared Virginia to the plight of a tenant being caught between two landlords and said, "It should not pledge itself to the party which had successfully established its right." Lincoln wanted the legislature to come together "and to vote to restore Virginia to the Union, and recall her soldiers from the Confederate army." Prominent Richmond lawyer Gustavus A. Myers said that the legislature could be convened. Lincoln promised to make his final decision at City Point.[176]

Wednesday, April 5

This was a rather quiet day. The morning was spent aboard the *Malvern* in various meetings. After the President had eaten breakfast, General Edward H. Ripley came aboard ship. With him was a man dressed in a Confederate uniform. Ripley and the President chatted in the cabin while the other gentleman waited outside. Ripley had come to warn the President about a possible assassination attempt. He related that the man in the hall was a Confederate deserter who had worked at the Torpedo Bureau in Richmond. Rumors were rampant that an attempt would be made on Lincoln's life. The two had come to warn the President. Would he see the man outside?

While Ripley spoke, Lincoln dropped his head and rubbed his chin. Slowly and sadly, he replied, "No, General Ripley." Lincoln said he appreciated the concern and warning. However, he must continue on the course he had charted. Lincoln concluded by saying, "I cannot bring myself to believe that any human lives who would do me any harm."[177]

After Ripley departed, General Weitzel arrived with Judge Campbell and Gustavus A. Myers. They met in the cabin of the *Malvern*. For an hour, they discussed the items necessary to restore Virginia to the Union. Lincoln referred to the three conditions he had stated earlier at Hampton Roads.

Not long after Campbell and Myers departed, Lincoln had a visitor. It was a negative situation. A slovenly-looking man, dressed in gray homespun, came to the landing. He held a piece of wood in his hand, almost like a club. He demanded to come aboard. The officer on deck inquired as to the nature of the visit. The answer was, "None of your business. I want to see Abraham Lincoln." Then he added, "You tell Abraham Lincoln Duff Green wants to see him." The officer conveyed the message to the cabin, where Crook, Porter and Weitzel were meeting with the President. Porter wanted to send the man away. However, Lincoln said, "Let him come on board. Duff is an old friend of mine."

This was against Porter's better judgment. The visitor glared at the "Stars and Stripes" and carried his piece of wood. Porter told him to come in a respectful manner and to throw away the wood.

With that, Green sneered and spoke of "man clothed in brief authority." He berated Porter and spoke of Lincoln's royalty. Green finally threw away the stick but said, "Is he afraid of assassination? Tyrants generally get into that condition." Porter thought the man was insane. In our day, a person like this would get nowhere near the President. Porter urged Lincoln not to see Green. "Let him come down," Lincoln replied. "He always was a little queer. I sha'nt mind him."

When Green entered the cabin, Mr. Lincoln extended his hand. Green refused it and scolded the President, ending his tirade with the words, "I do not know how God and your conscience will let you sleep at night after being guilty of the notorious crime of setting the niggers free." Then he stated the real reason for his coming. Green wanted a pass to leave the area. Lincoln instructed General Weitzel to issue a pass. Green took it without saying thank you or goodbye.

After Green left, Lincoln prepared to return to City Point. At 11:30 a.m., the tug pulled out. It was a lovely, spring-like day. At Dutch Gap, the barge proceeded around the five-mile bend in the river. Eight sailors pulled the barge through the channel. It had been dug by General Ben Butler's command in an effort to bypass the Confederate batteries on the bluffs. Lincoln inquired as to how many men lost their lives constructing the canal. He was told 140. Lincoln and Porter discussed Butler's military ability. Lincoln remarked that he was better at running cotton mills than as a "boss engineer." En route to City Point, the Presidential party stopped to visit the captured Confederate ram *Texas*.

Reaching City Point in the middle of the afternoon, Lincoln saw a transport ship in the harbor containing nearly one thousand Confederate prisoners. The POWs crowded on the deck to see the President. Prior to their capture, they were starving. Now their captors were feeding them beef and bread. When the President was rowed ashore, the Confederates cried, "That's Old Abe....Give the old fellow three cheers." Lincoln felt sorry for them. He looked forward to the day when they could return home.

As always, Lincoln proceeded to the telegraph office to see if there were any messages. There was one from Secretary Seward about some important items and asking when Lincoln would be returning to Washington. The President remained at the telegraph office for several hours, talking with Lieutenant Colonel Bowers and General Collis. The general was in command of the City Point garrison. He remarked that he had a guest, General Rufus Barringer. He had been captured a few days earlier and was awaiting transportation to a prison camp.

Barringer had heard that the President was at City Point and expressed a desire to meet him. Collis mentioned this fact to Lincoln. The President readily agreed. "Do you know, I have never seen a live rebel general in full uniform?"

Collis left the telegraph office and went to get Barringer. When Collis and his prisoner arrived, Lincoln rose to greet the Southern general and invited him to sit down. However, there was but one chair in the room, and Barringer remained standing. Lincoln studied his visitor and said, "Barringer, Barringer, from North Carolina....General were you ever in Congress?"

Barringer replied that he had not been a member of that august body but said, "That was my brother, sir."

With this, Lincoln laughed. "Well, well! Do you know that brother of yours was my chum in Congress? Yes sir, we sat at the same desk and ate at the same table. He was a Whig and so was I. He was my chum and I was fond of him. And you are his brother, eh? Well! Well, shake again." And the two men shook hands warmly. Additional chairs were brought into the room, and the two had a long conversation. They discussed Congressional days, the present conflict and the merits of various generals. Lincoln, as always, flavored his conversation with colorful anecdotes. Several times, General Barringer made an effort to leave, but Lincoln kept on speaking.

Lincoln said, "I suppose they will send you to Washington, and there I have no doubt they will put you in the old Capitol prison....I have a powerful friend in Washington....Now I want you to take this card of introduction to him." When the President finished writing and drying the ink with a blotter, he held the card up to the light and read it. The card was addressed to Secretary of War Stanton:

> *This is General Barringer of the Southern army. He is the brother of a very dear friend of mine. Can you do anything to make his detention in Washington as comfortable as possible under the circumstances?*
>
> *LINCOLN*[178]

Barringer tried to express his gratitude, but he was speechless. When he and Collis got outside, Barringer broke down and wept.

Lincoln remained at the telegraph office. He chatted with General Patrick and others. While he was in the office, a message came from Secretary Stanton that Secretary Seward had been seriously injured in a carriage accident. His shoulder bone was severely damaged, and his head and face were badly bruised. Stanton urged Mr. Lincoln to return to Washington as quickly as possible. In the same message, there was the news that Mrs. Lincoln and some of her friends had left Washington during the morning hours; Lincoln was troubled by the news of Seward's injuries. They were respected friends. However, he did not feel it was necessary to return to Washington. In regard to Mrs. Lincoln, it would have been best for her to remain in Washington, but since she was on the way, he would have to make the best of it.

Late at night, before going to sleep, Lincoln decided to check in on Tad, who was sleeping in the adjoining room along with William Crook. The guard awoke, terrified to find a tall, "white, ghostly figure hovering over him—Abraham Lincoln dressed in a nightgown." Recovering from his scare, Lincoln and Crook discussed the day's events. They spoke in subdued tones so as not to awaken Tad. Lincoln told Crook about the experience with Duff Green. He noted that Green was angry but would probably get over it. As he got ready to return to his own quarters, Lincoln said, "Good night, and a good night's rest, Crook."[179]

THURSDAY, APRIL 6

Mr. Lincoln spent the morning on the *River Queen*. He ate and read dispatches delivered from the telegraph office on shore. He contemplated the action he would take in regard to Virginia and the convening of the legislature. He spent time alone. He would soon have some visitors though. Mrs. Lincoln and her guests were returning to City Point.[180]

The President's wife had departed from Washington at 11:00 a.m. on April 5, aboard the *Monhassett*. The ship had pulled into Fort Monroe for the night. When she heard of Secretary's Seward's accident, she became panicky. Mary was afraid that Abe would dash back to Washington. She sent a hurried note urging him to remain at City Point until she arrived with her guests. In the meantime, Lincoln learned that Seward's injuries were not life threatening, so he decided to remain at City Point and await further military and political events.[181]

The *Monhassett* docked at noon. Mrs. Lincoln and her guests came aboard the *River Queen*. She had brought her seamstress, Elizabeth Keckley, along, as well as seven guests: Senator Charles Sumner of Massachusetts; a French nobleman by the name of Marquis de Chambrun; Attorney General James Speed; Judge William T. Otto; and Secretary of the Interior and Mrs. James Harlan and their daughter, Mary. The President greeted them and then took them below decks, where he and Secretary Seward had discussed peace with the Confederate commissioners. He showed which chairs the participants had occupied. He then shared some of General Grant's late communiqués from the front. He even went to an adjoining room to obtain maps to show them. Then he pointed out Confederate and Union positions and stated that if all went well, the Confederate armies would be forced to surrender. Chambrun noted that he talked without pride or vanity, but with the feeling that soon it would all be over.[182]

Next, Mr. Lincoln described his visit to Richmond. Mary immediately expressed disappointment that he had gone to Richmond without her. She wanted to see the city. Arrangements were then made to carry Mrs. Lincoln and her guests to Richmond. The group wanted the President to go with them. However, he declined. He was more interested in remaining at City Point for updates on the military situation. As soon as the touring party had gone, Lincoln went ashore and proceeded to the telegraph office. He sent a message to General Weitzel in Richmond informing him as to his wishes about the Virginia legislature:

Major General Weitzel City Point
Richmond, Va.
April 6, 1865

It has been intimated to me that the gentleman who have acted as the Legislature of Virginia, in support of the rebellion, many may now desire to assemble at Richmond, and take measures to withdraw the Virginia troops, and other support from resistance to the General government. If they attempt it, give them permission and protection, until, if at all, they attempt some action hostile to the United States, in which case you will notify them and give them reasonable time to leave; & at the end of which time, arrest any who may remain. Allow Judge Campbell to see this, but do not make it public. Yours & c.

A. Lincoln[183]

A message was also sent to General Grant informing him of the sessions with Judge Campbell and the President's decision about the legislature. Lincoln noted that Grant was "pretty effectually withdrawing the Virginia troops from opposition to the government. Nothing I have done, or probably shall do, is to delay, hinder, or interfere with you in your work."

April 6 brought the Union nearer victory; for the South it brought another day nearer defeat. At sunrise, A.A. Humphrey's Second Corps attacked John Gordon's men. The action continued over a fourteen-mile stretch of land. The Confederates fought fiercely, but there were simply too many blue coats. Heavy fighting occurred at High Bridge, so called because of the bridge built on piers, sixty feet above the narrow river. The bridge was important to the Confederate escape route. The Confederates were able to defend it for another day.[184]

Additional troubles followed the Confederates armies. There were communication problems, and John Gordon did not receive word about a change of wagon routes. Meanwhile, George Custer and George Crook were advancing rapidly. R.S. Ewell deployed his men along Little Sayler's Creek. For a while, Ewell held his ground. But then it was simply too many, too much—too many Union soldiers and too much Yankee firepower. Gordon's command along Sayler's Creek was overwhelmed. Ewell and Gordon lost nearly eight thousand men, many of them captured. This represented about one-third of the troops who had left Amelia and Jetersville. Six Confederate generals were captured, including Ewell. The end of the Army of Northern Virginia was very near.

Just when Mr. Lincoln should have been able to relate to the significance of the military situation, there was more news. His wife had arrived, and then later in the day, Vice President Andrew Johnson and Preston King arrived as well. Lincoln was seated in the telegraph office playing with kittens when the news arrived. A member of the *Malvern*'s crew informed Admiral Porter that the vice president was aboard the flagship and that he and King wanted to pay their respects to the President. Admiral Porter was surprised at the President's reaction:[185]

> *I never saw such a change in any one in my life as took place in Mr. Lincoln at this announcement. He jumped up from his chair where he had been playing with the kittens and rushed up to the door where the young officer was delivering his message. The President was greatly excited…he was almost frantic. "Don't let these men come into my presence. I won't see them. Send them away. They have no business here, any way; no right to come down here without my permission. I won't see them now.…I don't care what you do with them, nor where you send them, but don't let them come near me."*[186]

Porter had never seen the President so agitated. The admiral told the President that his wishes would be carried out. He instructed the junior officer to tell Commodore William Radford, "The President could receive no one today or tomorrow." Radford could give them fine liquors or take them anywhere they wished, but the President would not see Johnson and King. Lincoln did not want other politicians there to hinder him or the peace process.

Lincoln spent the rest of the evening in the telegraph office and then retired to the *Malvern*. Johnson and King remained at City Point over night and then traveled to Richmond the next day.[187]

Friday, April 7

With just one more week left in his earthly pilgrimage, Mr. Lincoln completed his second full week at City Point. He had breakfast with Admiral Porter on the *Malvern* and then went ashore, back to the telegraph office.

Soon a message came from U.S. Grant dated April 6. It contained the news of Sheridan's victory at Sayler's Creek with his cavalry and two divisions of infantry. "Little Phil" had captured six Confederate generals, several thousand enemy soldiers, fourteen cannons and a large number of wagons. Sheridan was continuing his pursuit of the Army of Northern Virginia. Sheridan said, "If the thing is pressed, I think Lee will surrender." Lincoln was pleased with the communiqué. His reply to Grant was a simple, "Let the thing be pressed." Soon additional messages concerning the news of Union progress came from Generals George G. Meade, Andrew Humphreys and Horatio Wright. The dispatchers brought more details of the victory at Sayler's Creek, which in reality was Lee's last military stand. After reading the messages, the President forwarded them to Secretary Stanton.[188]

Later in the morning, Assistant Secretary of War Charles Anderson Dana found Mr. Lincoln in a very good mood. The President showed Dana a copy of the peace proposal he had given Judge Campbell, along with the copy of the order he had given to General Weitzel, permitting the Rebel legislature to convene. Lincoln also remarked on the fast progress Sheridan was making at the battle front.[189]

Still later, Mrs. Lincoln and her guests returned from Richmond. The President invited them to accompany him to Petersburg. At about noon, a train headed for Petersburg. The Presidential party was in a special car. Some of the black waiters from the *River Queen* were also with them. Lincoln had no prejudice and invited the waiters to sit with the dignitaries.

Already, Union engineers had reopened the railroad directly into Petersburg. The trip took just about thirty minutes. Those on board the train saw the devastation in Petersburg. There "was the destructive hand of war… deserted houses, and ransacked stores."[190]

Crowds of black people greeted the arrival of the train. They cheered loudly because they realized it was Lincoln who had preserved and brought them freedom. A little black boy entered the President's car and offered to tote his belongings. Lincoln inquired as to the meaning of the word *tote*. Both the boy and Senator Sumner discussed the definition of the word.

A carriage arrived for the President. He took a few moments to shake hands with some in the crowd and then rode to Union headquarters at Centre Hill Mansion. While the rest of the group toured the elegant structure, Lincoln conferred with General George Hartsuff. He had met the general earlier when he visited him in Frederick on October 4, 1862. At that time, Hartsuff was recovering from wounds received at Antietam. Lincoln wanted to know the feeling of Petersburg's white population. Hartsuff talked about paying rent to the owners of Centre Hill. Lincoln looked at the holes in the walls made by shells and declared that the Federal batteries had "made rent enough here already."[191]

When the visit to Centre Hill concluded, there was a brief carriage ride of Petersburg, sort of a tour. General Hartsuff showed his guest the magnificent tree he had seen a few days earlier.

Lincoln shared with those in the carriage the news that Hartsuff said that white "animosity in the town is abating." The inhabitants had accepted the fact "of the final downfall of the Confederacy, and the abolition of slavery." Lincoln realized that there was still much to do. "But every day brings new reason for confidence in the future."

The return trip to City Point was slow. At one bend in the rails, the President noticed a terrapin basking in the sun. He gave the order for the train to stop and asked a crew member to bring the creature inside. The President and Tad were delighted with the creature and played with it "for the remainder of the ride."

A quiet evening was spent on board the *River Queen*. The guests were joined by two other Congressmen who had traveled to City Point, Elihu B. Washburne and James G. Blaine. They found Mr. Lincoln "in perfect health and exuberant spirits." The President spoke at length about his trip to Richmond and shared stories.[192]

Before the evening concluded, Washburne said that he hoped to visit General Grant before he returned to Washington. Lincoln asked if he would be so kind as to deliver a letter to his son Robert. Washburne naturally said yes, and before going to bed, Mr. Lincoln wrote a letter to his son.

While Lincoln was making his second visit to Petersburg, the Army of Northern Virginia had left Amelia around noon on April 5. Lee knew the Yankees were at Jetersville. Union scouts had been captured. The riders carried important dispatches. Union cavalry, as well as infantry, were at Jetersville.

Lee realized the impossibility of breaking through. Somehow, the Confederate chieftain had to try to get around the Union army. Lee's men needed food and supplies, otherwise they were finished.

Therefore, Lee set his columns in motion to the north. He hoped to pass Rice's Station on the Southside Railroad, seven miles northwest of Burkeville. Once he reached the station, Lee could be supplied by rail from Lynchburg and then perhaps continue to the west or possibly move south to Danville and still endeavor to link up with Johnston's army. However, it was a race with time, and his men were hungry and tired. The Army of Northern Virginia marched throughout the afternoon into the evening. Darkness fell.

The rains commenced, and still the hungry, tired men tramped the muddy roads. Exhaustion and hunger began to take a heavy toll. Many fell by the wayside. Some left the marching column to seek food or perhaps to sleep. The Army of Northern Virginia was dwindling. Later, when the Federals followed, they found the roads littered with discarded weapons, blankets, frying pans and more. And the roads behind the main column were filled with deserters, stragglers and men who could no longer continue. They were starved and exhausted. The men in the Army of Northern Virginia were "weary, sick, and hungry."

Saturday, April 8

The war was drawing to a close, as was Lincoln's visit to City Point. For fifteen days, Mr. Lincoln "had sojourned" at the large Union supply depot at City Point. He had not meant to stay that long, but he lingered in the hopes of being there for the moment of final victory. However, all things must come to an end, and he concluded that now it was time to return to Washington and the White House. Thus he informed Admiral Porter that he would depart at the close of the day.

Early in the morning, he went ashore to give Elihu Washburne the letter he had written to Robert. Washburne felt the President looked in fine spirits. A few moments later, Lincoln observed his last review at City Point.

At noon, Mr. Lincoln, Mary and a few guests journeyed to the Depot Field Hospital. This was a mile distant. He wanted to visit the sick and the wounded. Chief Medical Officer Edward B. Dalton met the President and invited him to tour the facilities. Lincoln declined, saying he wanted to see the troops. The President said, "Gentlemen, you know better than I how to conduct these hospitals, but I have come here to take by the hand the men who have achieved our glorious victories."

Mr. Lincoln then went to each hospital ward. He began his visits in the Fifth Corps hospital. At each place, those who were able to get out of bed and stand stood in line outside the barracks to shake the hand of the President of the United States. Then at each ward, the President went inside to speak with those too ill or too badly wounded to rise from their hospital beds. The President grasped the hand of each. The President greeted them and inquired as to their progress. He told the wounded that he expected the war to end within six weeks.[193]

The man of compassion, the man who thrust aside to rescue a puppy and a pig, now turning aside to grasp the hands of the wounded, the men who had bought victory at a great price, the troops who had saved the Union. This was "Father Abraham" at his best. The troops were honored by his visit, and he was honored by their "full measure of devotion" to the Union and to liberty.

Any writer is grateful for the research and the work of others. *Lincoln at City Point* by Donald C. Pfanz is a classic. We share his words about the continuation of Lincoln's visits to the hospitals:

> *Lincoln moved tirelessly from one tent to another for more than five hours in an effort to meet each patient then in the Depot Hospital. With him went an entourage of officers dressed in gold braid and dancing plumes. Their resplendent attire and cheerful dispositions struck many as inappropriate to the somber hospital setting. To Adelaide Smith, a volunteer nurse at the Ninth Corps hospital, the party "seemed so gay and careless that I felt a sort of contempt for them, where so many were groaning with wounds." She took particular offense at a lady dressed "in rich garb" who walked through the hospital "leaning on the arm of a Congressman"—an unmistakable reference to Mary Lincoln and Charles Sumner. With callous indifference to the feelings of those around her, Mrs. Lincoln noted the aesthetic shortcomings of the hospital and at one point suggested that a greenhouse be constructed on the grounds. When her companion expressed concern about the cost of such an undertaking, she replied disdainfully, "What of the expense?" Smith found the First Lady's arrogance so distasteful that she retired to her tent, "sick of folly—sick of fashion—sick of that species of my sex which trailed costly silks and laces in the dry dust," yet who refused to lift a finger to help those in need.*
>
> *Lincoln saw none of this; he was far too busy moving from one soldier to the next, shaking hands and offering words of condolence and hope. The surgeons who accompanied him on his rounds feared he would exhaust himself and urged him to stop, but he refused to slacken his pace. "I must see as many of them as possible," he insisted, "it may be long before I shall again have opportunity to shake hands with a wounded soldier." The only time he paused was to tarry at the bedside of seriously sick or wounded patients. One fellow, weak from disease, opened his eyes and found the President leaning over him. When he asked with feeble voice, "Is this Father Abraham?" Lincoln smiled and assured him it was.*
>
> *A few of the interviews conducted by the President were quite moving. In the hospital of the Ninth Army Corps, he halted beside the cot of Captain*

Charles H. Houghton of the 14th New York Heavy Artillery. The gallant 22-year old officer had been wounded three times at the Battle of Fort Stedman and as a result had lost his left leg. Lincoln put his hand to the young man's feverish brow, then leaned over and gently kissed him on the cheek. Tears came to his eyes when doctors pulled back the sheets to reveal the ghastly, unhealed stump. "You must live!" he cried, "Poor boy, you must live!" From the cot came the whispered reply, "I intend to, sir." In another instance Lincoln came upon a young man on the point of death. Two friends kept vigil at the man's side—one sat beside him and held his hand while the other read in hushed tones from the Scriptures. As members of his party looked on, Lincoln sat down quietly and took hold of the patient's free hand. At his touch, the dying man half opened his eyes and smiled faintly. A few moments later, the lad expired.[194]

During the visits, a member of the Sanitary Commission sought to prevent the President from entering some of the tents. Mr. Lincoln wanted to know why. The attendant replied, "They contain sick rebel prisoners."

"That is just where I do want to go," stated Mr. Lincoln. And before anyone could stop him, the President was inside the tents chatting with the wounded Confederates. He exemplified his words "With malice toward none."[195]

The President spent some time with Colonel Henry Benbow. The thirty-six-year-old officer had commanded a Confederate brigade at the Battle of Five Forks. He had been shot in both hips and then taken as a prisoner of war. Benbow never forgot the President's visit:

I was lying on my back, my knees drawn up and my hands folded across my breast. Looking him in the face as he stood with extended hand, I said, "Mr. President, do you know to whom you offer your hand?" "I do not," he replied. "Well," said I, "you offer your hand to a Confederate Colonel who has fought you as hard as he could for four years." "Well," said he, "I hope a Confederate Colonel will not refuse me his hand." "No sir," I replied, "I will not," and I clasped his hand in both of mine.[196]

Lincoln and Benbow visited for about ten minutes. When he departed, he took Benbow's hand and expressed the wish for Benbow's rapid recovery and reunification with his loved ones.

Lincoln also visited with some of the nurses. One of the angels of mercy was Helen Gibson, the daughter of a very wealthy family from Massachusetts. She left the comforts of her home to care for the sick and wounded. Her quarters were in a small room adjoining the kitchen. The room consisted of a bed, a small table and several tree stumps that served as chairs; a Bible rested on the table. Miss Gibson then showed the President a small booklet she had found in the pocket of a German soldier who had died in one of the Ninth Corps hospitals a few days earlier. Lincoln scanned the pages of the book and lamented the fate of the owner.[197]

Late in the afternoon, Mr. Lincoln finished his tours of the various hospitals. He had shaken hands with nearly five thousand soldiers. He was exhausted. His hand and arm pained and jumped. When a doctor suggested he must have a sore arm, Lincoln grabbed an axe, raised it and held it at an angle without any quiver to his arm. He was tired, though, and told Mary he wished to go to bed early.[198]

This was not possible, as Mrs. Lincoln had planned a reception aboard the *River Queen*. She had invited some of the prominent officers, politicians and their wives. The servants were busy decorating a large room. Elizabeth Keckley said, "It looked like an enchanted floating palace."[199] Guests began arriving at dark. Conspicuous from the guest list was Vice President Andrew Johnson. The relationship between Lincoln and Johnson was very cool.

Also absent was Mrs. Julia Grant. Mrs. Lincoln was slow to forget real or imagined slights. She had been unable to forgive Mrs. Grant for siding with Mary Ord during one of the Presidential reviews. Julia, in turn, was offended because Mrs. Lincoln had not invited her on the excursion to Petersburg on April 6.

Not to be outdone, Mrs. Grant also held a party on the *Mary Martin*, inviting an army band to play. She sailed downriver. When the *Martin* returned, the gala on the *River Queen* was at its height. Mrs. Grant had the ship sail across the *Queen*'s bow while the band played, "Now Do You Remember Me?"[200] However, those on board the *River Queen* were unaware of events transpiring outside.

Twice during the evening, Lincoln asked the band to play "La Marseillaise," the French anthem. It had been banned by the French government, but Lincoln wanted it played for his guest the Marquis de Chambrun. One of Lincoln's favorites was "Dixie." He asked Chambrun if he was familiar with the song. He replied that he was not. Therefore, the President ordered the band to play "Dixie," and jokingly said, "That tune is now Federal Property."[201]

The festivities concluded at 10:00 p.m. The President made a short speech and said goodnight to each of the guests. Then he gave Captain Bradford orders to start for Washington. Soon the engine was humming, and the *River*

Queen cast off, accompanied by the *Bat*. Lincoln remained on deck for a long time, gazing back at City Point and contemplating the last two weeks. Chambrun stood at his side, quietly observing the President, who seemed lost in his thoughts, even after City Point had disappeared from view.[202]

Palm Sunday, April 9

While the Presidential party slept, the *River Queen* proceeded northward. Shortly after dawn, the vessel docked at Fort Monroe. Some of the officers went ashore to pick up mail and check telegrams. Captain Barnes requested a few moments with Mr. Lincoln. He wanted to say goodbye.

Barnes, some junior officers and a small contingent of sailors had been detached to guard and provide additional security for the President. Now that the *Queen* was ready to enter the Chesapeake, it was time for Barnes to provide escort, all the way to Washington from the *Bat*. Lincoln firmly clasped the naval officer's hand. He expressed his gratitude for the fine care and protection. In a teasing manner, Lincoln joked about the navy having it better than the foot soldiers.[203]

The *Queen* and *Bat* then got underway for the last segment of the journey. Lincoln spent the rest of the day below deck, conversing with other passengers. Particularly, he and Chambrun discussed France's meddling into Mexico's internal affairs. Chambrun asked about the possibility of war after the surrender of the Confederate armies. Lincoln said, "We have had enough war....Rest assured that during my second term, there will be no more fighting."

Lincoln then changed the conversation. Instead of discussing the occupation of the South, the treatment of Jefferson Davis and possible war with Mexico, he began to read aloud from Shakespeare. Many of the verses were from *Macbeth*. Chambrun noticed the President's selections and his tone of voice. He placed great emphasis on Duncan's assassination:

> *Duncan is in his grave,*
> *After life's fitful fever, he sleeps well.*[204]

Lincoln paused while reading. Perhaps he had a feeling of foreboding. Chambrun stated that in the previous days, the President exhibited "a vague and deep sadness." He seemed burdened. Even when he laughed, he would quickly lapse into deep thought. No one ever found what was going through the President's mind.

As the shade of night fell and the sun slipped behind the western horizon, darkness had fallen with finality to the Confederacy. Great news awaited the President when the *River Queen* docked. As the journey neared its end, Lincoln and Chambrun went topside and stood on the *Queen*'s deck. To the starboard side was Fort Washington and on the port side, Mount Vernon. Chambrun began speaking of and comparing Mount Vernon and Springfield. Lincoln said suddenly, "Springfield, how happy I shall be four years hence to return there in peace and tranquility."

Shortly after 6:00 p.m., the *River Queen* docked at the Navy Yard. He had special words of thanks for Charles Penrose. Then it was on to the White House. Lincoln's wartime travels were over, and he was entering his last week on earth. Soon he would be on another train, returning to his beloved Springfield.

GLEANINGS

Origin of the Trip to City Point

U.S. Grant felt that if Mr. Lincoln wanted to come to City Point, he'd come regardless of an invitation. Mrs. Grant persisted, saying that she did not believe he would come without an invitation. By this time, Robert Lincoln was serving on Grant's staff as a captain and aide. One morning, Mrs. Grant asked Robert what he thought about the commander in chief coming to City Point. Robert replied that he thought his parents would come if they were sure they would not be intruding. That settled the matter. Grant walked to the telegraph and sent the following message:

> *His Excellency A. Lincoln: Can you not visit City Point for a day or two? I would like very much to see you, and I think the rest would do you good.*
>
> *Respectfully yours, etc.*
> *U.S. GRANT, LIEUTENANT GENERAL*

The response was rapid. That evening, March 29, 1865, U.S. Grant received an eager message:

> *Your kind invitation received. Had already thought of going immediately after the next rain. Will go sooner if any reason for it. Mrs. L. and a few others will probably accompany me. Will notify you of exact time, once it shall be fixed upon.*
>
> *A. LINCOLN*

Thus the die was cast. The two telegrams opened the door to the last days of Mr. Lincoln, as well as a meaningful time in the life of the wartime president.

President Lincoln met with General McClellan at Harrison's Landing on the Berkeley Westover Plantations on July 8, 1862. This was the home of the Harrison family from whom President William Henry Harrison was descended. The father of the former President had been a signer of the Declaration of Independence.

It was en route to Berkeley that the steamer ran aground. While waiting to be released, the Presidential family took a swim in the James River.

Arriving late, Mr. Lincoln reviewed the troops in the moonlight and again the next day at Westover. Berkeley had also claimed to have had both Washington and Lincoln as its distinguished guests. However, McClellan had his headquarters in the woods, and it is uncertain that Lincoln ever entered the house. Also, some strategy meetings were held on board the steamer. Berkeley is a most historical spot. Ten presidents have been there. Some claim that the first Thanksgiving was held on the grounds in 1619. And some claim that the haunting refrains of taps were composed nearby. Berkeley Plantation is open to the public. Westover is open on a limited basis.

A SATURDAY TIRADE, MARCH 24, 1865

Some feel that both Mary Todd and Abraham Lincoln were somewhat withdrawn and emotionally detached. Both had lost their mothers in death in their early years. Some feel that both Abe and Mary had felt abandoned. Lincoln was not close to his father, and Mary's father had sixteen children by two wives. She also seems to have been bipolar—emotionally one moment in the attic and the next in the basement. This disorder seems to have been prevalent in the Todd family.

Regardless, Mary put on quite a display at City Point, becoming upset with Julia Grant, Mrs. Ord and Mrs. Griffin. The latter was the subject of a Saturday tirade.

The Lincolns, the Grants and others had taken an hourlong train trip to Patrick Street Station in Petersburg. Upon arrival, Lincoln and Grant mounted horses, while Colonel Adam Badeau drove a carriage with Mrs. Lincoln and Julia Grant.

Badeau casually mentioned that all women, with the exception of Mrs. Charles Griffin, had been ordered to the rear—she had received special permission to remain at the front from President Lincoln. This angered Mary. She screamed, "Do you mean my husband saw her alone?" She demanded and tried to get out of the carriage. However, Mrs. Grant was able to calm her. She always sought to keep her Abe at arm's length from other women.

Colonel Badeau feared the worst. However, upon arrival at Meade's headquarters, Meade stated that it was he, not Mr. Lincoln, who gave permission to Mrs. Griffin to remain.

LINCOLN THEN AND NOW

MARYLAND

The Antietam-Sharpsburg area, a pastoral place, remains much the same as in 1862. The Showman farms on Mills Road are still lovely dwellings, tastefully cared for by their owners. These were the headquarters of George B. McClellan and Ambrose Burnside. Some of the acreage has been sold for farmettes. Mills Road is reached by going south on Burnside Bridge Road.

The Grove farm, Mount Airy, still graces farmland west of Sharpsburg. This is the location of the famed group picture of Lincoln and Fitz John Porter's staff at Antietam, as well as the possible birthplace of the Gettysburg Address. The threatened development of the property led to a wakeup call for the State of Maryland. These three properties are privately owned.

The Dunker Church blew down in a windstorm in the 1920s but has since been rebuilt. The Pry farm and some acreage are owned by the National Park Service and, in partnership with the National Medical Museum in Frederick, are opened as a Civil War hospital site.

PENNSYLVANIA

Gettysburg, of course, occupies a unique position in American history. One can visit the train station where Lincoln arrived on November 18 and then departed on November 19. At the Square, or Diamond, there is the restored home of David Wills, where Lincoln stayed the night of November 18. Then there is the National Cemetery and the site of the Gettysburg Address. Likewise, there is the Presbyterian church where Lincoln attended a lecture on the afternoon of the nineteenth.

VIRGINIA

Lincoln was at Aquia Landing in the spring of 1863. The site is at the end of Virginia Route 608 and can be reached via Virginia 628. Watch for signs on I-95. There is also a marker on U.S. 1, just north of Stafford.

Belle Plain was another site visited by Lincoln. It is at the south side of Potomac Creek at the east end of Virginia 604. Lincoln reviewed seventeen thousand troops here along with Tad and Mary on April 9, 1863.

Fredericksburg is associated with George Washington and other noted Americans. However, in April 1862, Mr. Lincoln visited the Phillips house, which later burned, as well as Chatham, which now serves as headquarters for the Fredericksburg National Park. The visit came on May 23. Lincoln and Secretary Stanton met with the French foreign minister, along with General McDowell and Captain John Dahlgren. Chatham has claimed that it is the only place visited by both Lincoln and Washington.

Lincoln crossed the Rappahannock on a canal barge and pontoon bridge and then rode to the headquarters of General Marsena Patrick, located at the Farmers Bank, at the intersection of Princess Anne and George Streets.

Fort Monroe was known as the "Gibraltar of the Chesapeake Bay." Robert E. Lee had been the chief engineer during the construction. The Lees' first child was born at the fort. Lincoln was here in the spring of 1862, and the *River Queen* stopped for fresh water on March 24, 1865. After the war, the famed *River Queen* docked here, very proudly displaying its Lincoln room. Sadly, the famed vessel was destroyed by fire in Washington, D.C., in 1911. Mr. Lincoln made a triumphant entrance into Petersburg on April 3 and then Richmond on April 4. The Thomas

Wallace house, the headquarters of U.S. Grant, was located at 204 South Market Street. The home of Confederate general Roger Pryor was located on Washington Street. Lincoln also visited the headquarters of General George Hartsuff at Center Hill. The home is open to the public. It was Hartsuff whom Lincoln visited in Frederick.

NOTES

A Traveling Man

1. From Springfield, Mr. Lincoln took ten days to travel to Washington, stopping in Columbus, Indianapolis, Albany, Trenton and Philadelphia. In Baltimore, plans were changed due to a death threat. The funeral train in 1865 traversed the route in reverse.
2. For this writer, Sandburg's *Abraham Lincoln* is still the classic.
3. Cincinnati, Cleveland, Pittsburgh and Buffalo were also part of the journey. *Cincinnati Commercial*, February 16, 1861.
4. Monaghan, *Diplomat in Carpet Slippers*, 224.

Travels in 1862

5. The Washington Navy Yard seems to have been a favorite spot of Mr. Lincoln's. From time to time, it was the place of the beginning and ending of his journeys to Fort Monroe, Aquia Creek and Belle Plain.
6. From the *Diary of Rear Admiral John Dahlgren*. Inventor of the Dahlgren gun, he is also the man for whom Dahlgren Hall at the U.S. Naval Academy is named. After the war, the family owned the famed Mountain House on the National Road at Turner's Gap. Mrs. Dahlgren, a devout Catholic, erected a chapel in an effort to convert and educate local children.
7. Ibid.

8. *Fort Monroe in History*, pamphlet, 1970, National Park Service.

9. See Powell, *Lincoln Day by Day*, vol. 3. This is a must in tracing Lincoln's daily calendar.

10. Joseph Johnston was the Confederate commander during the early days of the 1862 Peninsula Campaign. After he was wounded, Robert E. Lee assumed command of the Army of Northern Virginia.

11. *Diary of Rear Admiral John Dahlgren*; James W. Hunnicutt, *Christian Banner*, May 24, 1862.

12. Otis, *Second Wisconsin Infantry*, 48.

13. Ibid., 48–49.

14. Ibid., 79.

15. Gibbon, *Reminiscences of the Civil War*, 32–33.

16. *New York Times*, June 26, 1862.

17. *National Intelligencer*, June 26, 1862.

18. *Utica Gazette*, June 25, 1862.

19. *New York Times*, June 26, 1862.

20. Ibid.; *National Intelligencer*, June 27, 1862.

21. *New York Tribune*, July 10, 1862.

22. Powell, *Lincoln Day by Day*, July 9–10, 1862.

23. *Washington Star*, July 11, 1862.

24. Lee wrote to President Jefferson Davis on September 3, 1862, stating that he believed this was the most advantageous time to go north.

25. See Murfin, *Gleam of Bayonets*, 19, and Sears, *Landscape Turned Red*.

26. *Hagerstown Torchlight*, September 1862.

27. See Carpenter, *Six Months at the White House*, 20–22.

28. Abraham Lincoln, the Emancipation Proclamation, National Archives.

29. Sandburg, *Abraham Lincoln*, 210.

30. See Delaplaine, *Lincoln's Companions on the Trip to Antietam*. The late judge and distinguished Frederick historian was the first to write on Lincoln's visit to Antietam.

31. See O'Connor, *Man Who Could Might Have Saved the Union*.

32. See Howard, *Autobiography of Oliver Otis Howard*.

33. *New York Herald*, October 3, 1862.

34. A.S. Williams letters to his daughters in Detroit, contained in Quaife, *From the Cannon's Mouth*, 136.

35. Hinkley, *Narrative of Service*, 63.

36. Brown, *Twenty Seventh Indiana Volunteer Infantry*, 270.

37. *New York Herald*, October 3, 1862.

38. Lord, *History of the Ninth New Hampshire Volunteers*, 145.

39. Lamon, *Recollections of Abraham Lincoln*, 141–45.

40. Ellis, *Leaves from the Diary of an Army Surgeon*, 300.

41. Dr. James Oliver, journal entry for October 3, 1862, copy in possession of the author.

42. Lord, *History of the Ninth New Hampshire Volunteers*, 146.

43. Joshua Chamberlain Papers.

44. From the papers of Louisa Grove, Grove Family Papers, author's collection.

45. *Cincinnati Commercial*, October 4, 1862.

46. Accounts from Lamon, *Recollections of Abraham Lincoln*.

47. Ibid.

48. Nevins, *Diary of Battle*, 33. The review was held either on the east side or west side of what is now Mondell Road.

49. Lord, *History of the Ninth New Hampshire Volunteers*, 149.

50. Hazel Pry Morena, interview by author, 1972.

51. *Valley Register*, October 10, 1862.

52. Alice Frazier Bouldin Papers.

53. Marvin, *Fifth Regiment Connecticut Volunteers*, 238.

54. Jacob Engelbrecht Diary.

55. *New York Tribune*, October 4, 1862.

56. Curtis, *Twenty-Fourth Michigan*, 200.

57. *Baltimore Sun*, October 5, 1862.

58. Dawes, *Service with the Sixth Wisconsin*, 129.

59. Ibid., 130.

Travels in 1863

60. Brooks, *Washington, D.C., in Lincoln's Time*, 146; *Sacramento Union*, April 12, 1863.

61. See Brooks, *Washington, D.C., in Lincoln's Time*.

62. Ibid., 50.

63. Bruce, *Twentieth Regiment of Massachusetts Volunteer Infantry*, 225.

64. Nevins, *Diary of Battle*, 171.

65. Ibid., 177.

66. Brooks, *Washington, D.C., in Lincoln's Time*, 49.

67. Ibid.

68. Ibid.

69. De Trobriand, *Four Years with the Army of the Potomac*, 427.

70. Brooks, *Washington, D.C., in Lincoln's Time*, 51.

71. See Sedgwick, *Correspondence of John Sedgwick, Major General*, 2 vols.

72. *Rochester Union*, April 8, 1863; Brooks, *Washington, D.C., in Lincoln's Time*, 55–60.

73. Brooks, *Washington, D.C., in Lincoln's Time*, 49.

74. Galwey and Nye, *Valiant Hours*, 80.

75. Johnson and Buel, *Battles and Leaders of the Civil War*, vol. 3, 121.

76. Bennett, *104ᵗʰ New York Infantry*, 147.

77. See Porter Farley, *Reminiscences*. He also wrote letters to the *Rochester Evening Express*. After the war, he became a physician and often wrote about his wartime experiences.

78. Galwey and Nye, *Valiant Hours*, 78.

79. Ibid.

80. Bruce, *Twentieth Regiment of Massachusetts Volunteer Infantry*, 227.

81. Gibbon, *Reminiscences of the Civil War*, 271.

82. Letter of David T. Morrill, chaplain of the Twenty-Sixth New Jersey, New Jersey Archives.

83. Pullen, *Twentieth Maine*, 72.

84. Brooks, *Washington, D.C., in Lincoln's Time*, 51.

85. Ibid., 55–60.

86. *Washington Star*, April 10, 1863.

87. Letter of Shattuck, quoted in Dawes, *Service with the Sixth Wisconsin*.

88. Dawes, *Service with the Sixth Wisconsin*, 132.

89. *Cincinnati Gazette*, April 1863.

90. See Buell, *Cannonneer*.

91. See Howard, *Autobiography of Oliver Otis Howard*.

92. Ibid.

93. Justus M. Sillman, a member of the Seventeenth Connecticut, in a letter to his family, April 1863, private collection.

94. William Wheeler, memory of Lincoln's visit, private collection.

95. Brown, *Twenty Seventh Indiana Volunteer Infantry*, 298.

96. Slocum, *Life and Services of Major General Henry Warner Slocum*, letter to wife on April 19, 1863.

97. A.S. Williams to his daughters, April 14, 1863, contained in Quaife, *From the Cannon's Mouth*.

98. Brown, *Twenty Seventh Indiana Volunteer Infantry*, 299.

99. Ibid., 300.

100. Ibid., 301.

101. Brooks, *Washington, D.C., in Lincoln's Time*, 59.

102. James Creole to Hiram Averall, April 1863, private collection.

103. Charles Morse letter, private collection.

104. George Breck letter, private collection.

105. Gibbon, *Reminiscences of the Civil War*, 424–25.

106. Brooks, *Washington, D.C., in Lincoln's Time*, 57–58.

107. Reorganization of the Army of Northern Virginia. See John W. Schildt's *Roads to Gettysburg*.

108. *Richmond Whig*, June 19, 1863.

109. Charles F. Benjamin, "Hooker's Appointment and Removal," in Johnson and Buel, *Battles and Leaders of the Civil War*, vol. 3, 239–43.

110. *Adams Sentinel*, July 7, 1863.

111. Powell, *Lincoln Day by Day*, November 8–15, 1863.

112. See Kunhardt, *New Birth of Freedom*, perhaps the best book covering the famed Gettysburg Address. See also Boritt, *Gettysburg Gospel*.

113. See Hay and Nicolay, *Abraham Lincoln*, 10 vols.

114. Lamon, *Recollections of Abraham Lincoln*, 69–79.

115. Powell, *Lincoln Day by Day*, November 16–19, 1863.

116. Gibbon, *Reminiscences of the Civil War*, 476.

117. Kunhardt, *New Birth of Freedom*, 297.

118. Powell, *Lincoln Day by Day*, November 19, 1863; Bates Diary, November 30, 1863.

119. *Southern Maryland News*, April 22, 2009.

Travels in 1864

120. *Washington Star*, June 17, 1864.

121. Ibid.

122. Porter, "Campaigning with Grant," 216–24.

123. *New York Herald*, June 25, 1864; Porter, "Campaigning with Grant," 216–24.

124. See Worthington, *Fighting for Time*.

125. *Washington Star*, August 1, 1864.

126. Gideon Welles Diary, August 2, 1864, 124; Worthington, *Fighting for Time*, 206.

127. Worthington, *Fighting for Time*, 206. See also the memoirs of U.S. Grant. Generals Grant and Sheridan met at the Thomas farm on the Monocacy Battlefields. The subject was total warfare, as well as a pincers movement. Grant was at Petersburg with Sheridan in the Shenandoah Valley.

Travels in 1865

128. Ward Hill Lamon was a primary source for Lincoln's visit to Antietam. Noah Brooks wrote extensively about Lincoln's visit with Joseph Hooker and the many reviews in the spring of 1863. Volumes have been written about the trip to Gettysburg. However, Donald C. Pfanz has done the scholarly work on Lincoln's trip to visit U.S. Grant at City Point in his *Petersburg Campaign: Abraham Lincoln at City Point*, March 20–April 9, 1865. Marquis de Chambrun traveled with Lincoln to City Point and included portions of those days in *Impressions of Lincoln in the Civil War*. He was invited to travel with Mary Lincoln to City Point on April 2 and recorded conversations with Lincoln on the return trip via the Chesapeake and Potomac. The writings of J.S. Barnes, the naval officer with Lincoln; William Crook, a White House guard; the diary of Admiral David Porter; and General Grant's autobiography are also helpful.

129. Abraham Lincoln, Second Inaugural Address, March 4, 1865, National Archives.

130. *Washington Star*, March 5, 1865.

131. Grant, *Personal Memoirs of Julia Dent Grant*, 145.

132. Pfanz, *Petersburg Campaign*, 23.

133. Ibid.

134. Barnes, "With Lincoln from Washington to Richmond," part 1, 515–24, 742–51.

135. Pfanz, *Petersburg Campaign*, 25.

136. Barnes, "With Lincoln from Washington to Richmond," part 1, 516.

137. Porter, "Campaigning with Grant," 546.

138. Powell, *Lincoln Day by Day*, 322.

139. Sandburg, *Abraham Lincoln*, vol. 4, 147.

140. Grant, *Personal Memoirs of Julia Dent Grant*, 146.

141. Ibid., 140–41.

142. Barnes, "With Lincoln from Washington to Richmond," part 1, 524.

143. Pfanz, *Petersburg Campaign*, 28; Powell, *Lincoln Day by Day*, 322–23.

144. Barnes, "With Lincoln from Washington to Richmond," part 1, 524.

145. Sandburg, *Abraham Lincoln*, 524.

146. Barnes, "With Lincoln from Washington to Richmond," part 1, 524.

147. Barnes, "With Lincoln from Washington to Richmond," part 2, 742. Officer Barnes wrote of his trips in two installments.

148. See Porter, "Campaigning with Grant," 422–23, and Sherman, *Memoirs of General William T. Sherman*, vol. 2, 325. General Sherman

wrote extensively of his admiration for President Lincoln and the 1865 conferences on the *River Queen*.

149. Sherman, *Memoirs of General William T. Sherman*, 326–27.

150. Ibid.

151. Porter, "Campaigning with Grant," 427.

152. Ibid.

153. Ibid.

154. Bates, *Lincoln in the Telegraph Office*, 344.

155. Ibid., 346.

156. *OR*, series I, vol. 46, part 3, 394.

157. The date of Lincoln's dream is uncertain. It was some time around March 31. Pfanz, *Petersburg Campaign*, 103; Sandburg, *Abraham Lincoln*, 224–25; and William Crook, who witnessed the President's mental state, point to April 1.

158. Crook, "Lincoln as I Knew Him" (1907), 519.

159. U.S. Grant's reports, March 31, 1865, *OR*, series I, vol. 46, part 3, 448.

160. Moore, *Moore's Complete Civil War Guide*, 41.

161. Ibid.

162. Barnes, "With Lincoln from Washington to Richmond," part 2, 526.

163. Moore, *Moore's Complete Civil War Guide*; Clement Sulivane, "The Fall of Richmond."

164. Porter, *Incidents and Anecdotes*, 283–84.

165. Ibid.

166. See Johnson, *Long Roll*.

167. Pryor, *My Day*, 257–58.

168. Moore, *Moore's Complete Civil War Guide*, 42.

169. Ibid.

170. Pfanz, *Petersburg Campaign*, 52.

171. Coffin, *Abraham Lincoln*, 601.

172. Porter, "Campaigning with Grant," 488–83.

173. See Campbell, *Reminiscences and Documents*; Pfanz, *Petersburg Campaign*, 106.

174. Campbell, *Reminiscences and Documents*, 107.

175. Coffin, *Boys of '61*, 510.

176. Campbell, *Reminiscences and Documents*, 107.

177. Sandburg, *Abraham Lincoln*, vol. 4, 247.

178. Collis, *Woman's War Record*, 62–70; Pfanz, *Petersburg Campaign*, 74–76.

179. Crook, "Lincoln as I Knew Him" (1907), 522.

180. Pfanz, *Petersburg Campaign*, 77.

181. Crook, "Lincoln as I Knew Him" (1906), 58–59.

182. Chambrun, *Impressions of Lincoln and the Civil War*, 27–28, 73, 74.

183. Telegram, Lincoln to Major General Weitzel, April 6, 1865, in Bates, *Lincoln in the Telegraph Office*.

184. Chambrun, *Impressions of Lincoln and the Civil War*, 73–77.

185. Porter, *Incidents and Anecdotes*, 287.

186. In addition to Julia Dent Grant's memoir, the reader is also referred to Grant, *In the Days of My Father*, and Grant, *Personal Memoirs of U.S. Grant*, 2 vols.

187. Pfanz, *Petersburg Campaign*, 80.

188. *Official Records of the Union and Confederate Navies*, series I, vol. 12, 176.

189. Ibid.

190. Chambrun, *Impressions of Lincoln and the Civil War*, 28.

191. Ibid., 29.

192. Ibid., 32.

193. Ibid., 78–80; Pfanz, *Petersburg Campaign*, 84–88; Powell, *Lincoln Day by Day*, 326–28.

194. Chambrun, *Impressions of Lincoln and the Civil War*, 30.

195. Powell, *Lincoln Day by Day*, 326.

196. Chambrun, *Impressions of Lincoln and the Civil War*, 78–80.

197. Ibid.

198. Ibid. See also Pfanz, *Petersburg Campaign*, 84–88.

199. Chambrun, *Impressions of Lincoln and the Civil War*, 80.

200. Grant, *Personal Memoirs of Julia Dent Grant*, 150; Barnes, "With Lincoln from Washington to Richmond," part 1, 524.

201. Grant, *Personal Memoirs of Julia Dent Grant*, 150–51.

202. Chambrun, *Impressions of Lincoln and the Civil War*, 34.

203. Ibid., 35; Sandburg, *Abraham Lincoln*, 195.

204. Pfanz, *Petersburg Campaign*, 90.

BIBLIOGRAPHY

Basic Works

Gary, Ralph. *Following in Lincoln's Footsteps: A Complete Annotated Reference to Hundreds of Sites Visited by Abraham Lincoln*. New York: Carroll & Graf, 2001. This is an amazing book, taking the reader state by state to Lincoln sites.

The Official Atlas of the Civil War. New York: T. Yoseloff, 1958.

Official Records of the Union and Confederate Navies in the War of the Rebellion. Washington, D.C.: Government Printing Office, 1894–1922.

Powell, Percy, ed. *Lincoln Day by Day. A Chronology, 1861–1865*. Vol. 3. Washington, D.C.: Lincoln Sesquicentennial Commission, 1960. This is a must for anyone following the footsteps of Lincoln.

War of the Rebellion: A Compilation of the Official Records of the Union and Confederate Armies. Parts I and II. Washington, D.C.: Government Printing Office, 1880–91.

Manuscripts, Letters, Diaries and Other Books

Alice Frazier Bouldin Papers. Frederick County Historical Society, Frederick, Maryland.

Atkinson, James. "Mr. Lincoln Visits His Army." *Civil War Times*, June 1972.

Barnes, John S. "With Lincoln from Washington to Richmond." *Appleton's Magazine* (May–June 1907).

————. "With Lincoln from Washington to Richmond." *Appleton's Magazine* 9, no. 6 (June 1907).

Basler, Roy P., ed. *The Collected Works of Abraham Lincoln*. 8 vols. New Brunswick, NJ: Rutgers University Press, 1953.

Bates, Donald Homer. *Lincoln in the Telegraph Office*. New York: Century Company, 1939.

Benjamin, Charles F. "Hooker's Appointment and Removal." In *Battles and Leaders of the Civil War*. Vol. 3. Edited by Robert Underwood Johnson and Clarence Clough Buel. New York: Century Company, 1887.

Bennett, Brian A. *The 104ᵗʰ New York Infantry*. Dayton, OH, 1992.

Boritt, Gabor. *The Gettysburg Gospel: The Lincoln Speech that Nobody Knows*. New York: Simon & Schuster, 2006.

Brooks, Noah. *Washington, D.C., in Lincoln's Time*. New York: Rinehart & Company, 1958.

Brown, Edmund. *The Twenty Seventh Indiana Volunteer Infantry in the War of the Rebellion, 1861 to 1865*. Gaithersburg, MD: Butternut Press, n.d.

Bruce, George. *The Twentieth Regiment of Massachusetts Volunteer Infantry*. Boston: Houghton Mifflin, 1906.

Buell, Augustus C. *The Cannoneer: Recollections of Service in the Army of the Potomac*. Albuquerque, NM: Battery A, 3ʳᵈ U.S. Artillery (Memorial), 1988.

Campbell, John A. *Reminiscences and Documents Relating to the Civil War during the Year 1865*. Baltimore, MD: J. Murphy, 1887.

Carpenter, F.B. *Six Months at the White House*. New York: Hurd and Houghton, 1867.

Catton, Bruce. *Mr. Lincoln's Army*. New York: Doubleday and Company, 1951.

Chambrun, Charles A.P. *Impressions of Lincoln and the Civil War: A Foreigner's Account*. New York, 1952. Later revised and titled *Personal Recollections of Mr. Lincoln*.

Coffin, Charles Carleton. *Abraham Lincoln*. New York: Harper & Brothers Publishers, 1893.

Collis, Septima. *A Woman's War Record, 1861–1865*. New York: G.P. Putnam and Sons, 1889.

Cook, Benjamin F. *History of the Twelfth Massachusetts Volunteers*. Charleston, SC: Nabu Press, 2010.

Cox, Jacob. *Military Reminiscences of the Civil War*. New York: C. Scribner's Sons, 1900.

Crook, William H. "Lincoln as I Knew Him." *Harpers Monthly* (1906 and 1907).

Curtis, Newton Martin. *From Bull Run to Chancellorsville*. New York, 1906.

Curtis, Orson B. *The Twenty-Fourth Michigan*. Detroit, MI: Winn & Hammond, 1891.

Dahlgren, Madeleine V. *Memoirs of Rear Admiral John A. Dahlgren, U.S. Navy by His Widow*. Boston: J.R. Osgood, 1882.

Dawes, Rufus. *Service with the Sixth Wisconsin Volunteers*. Marietta, OH: E.R. Alderman & Sons, 1890.

Delaplaine, Edward S. *Lincoln's Companions on the Trip to Antietam*. Harrogate, TN: Lincoln Memorial University Press, 1954.

De Trobriand, Regis. *Four Years with the Army of the Potomac*. Bethesda, MD: University Publications of America, 1994.

Ellis, Thomas T. *Leaves from the Diary of an Army Surgeon*. New York: J. Bradburn, 1863.

Engelbrecht, Jacob. *The Diary of Jacob Engelbrecht, 1818–1878*. Frederick, MD: Historical Society of Frederick County, 1976.

Farley, Porter. *Reminiscences of the 140th Regiment, New York State Volunteer Infantry*. N.p., 1878.

Galwey, Thomas, and Wilbur Sturtevant Nye. *The Valiant Hours*. Harrisburg, PA, 1961.

Gibbon, John. *Reminiscences of the Civil War*. New York, 1928.

Grant, Jesse R. *In the Days of My Father, General Grant*. New York: Harper and Bros., 1925.

Grant, Julia. *The Personal Memoirs of Julia Dent Grant*. New York: Putnam, 1975.

Grant, Ulysses Simpson. *Personal Memoirs of U.S. Grant*. 2 vols. Montreal: Dawson Bros., 1886.

The Grove Family Papers. Hagerstown, Maryland. Private collection.

Hay, John, and John G. Nicolay. *Abraham Lincoln: A History*. New York: Century Company, 1890.

Henry, J. Maurice. *History of the Church of the Brethren in Maryland*. Fort Wayne, IN: Allen County Public Library, n.d.

Hinkley, Julian W. *A Narrative of Service with the Third Wisconsin Infantry*. Madison, WI: Wisconsin Historical Commission, 1912.

Howard, Oliver Otis. *Autobiography of Oliver Otis Howard, Major General United States Army*. New York: Baker & Tayor, 1908.

Hunnicutt, James W. *Christian Banner*. May 24, 1862.

Hussey, George, and Todd William. *History of the Ninth Regiment, N.Y.S.M.—N.G.S.N.Y.* Bethesda, MD: University Publications of America, 1992.

The James Oliver Papers and Diary. Athol, Massachusetts, and Sharpsburg, Maryland. Personal collection.

Johnson, Charles. *The Long Roll*. Shepherdstown, WV: Carabelle Books, 1986.

Joshua Chamberlain Papers. Bowdoin College and the Library of Congress.

Keckley, Elizabeth Hobbs. *Behind the Scenes*. New York: National News Company, 1868.

Kunhardt, Philip B., Jr. *A New Birth of Freedom: Lincoln at Gettysburg*. Boston: Little, Brown, 1983.

Lamon, Ward Hill. *Recollections of Abraham Lincoln, 1847–1865*. Chicago: A.C. McClurg & Company, 1895.

Lane, David. *A Soldier's Diary, 1862–1865*. Charleston, SC: Nabu Press, 2010.

Lord, Edward O. *A History of the Ninth Regiment New Hampshire Volunteers*. Concord, NH: Republican Press Association, 1895.

MacNamara, Daniel. *The History of the Ninth Regiment, Massachusetts Volunteers Infantry*. Boston: E.B. Stillings & Company, 1899.

Marvin, Edwin E. *The Fifth Regiment Connecticut Volunteers*. Hartford, CT: Wiley, Waterman and Eaton, 1889.

Monaghan, Jay. *Diplomat in Carpet Slippers: Abraham Lincoln Deals with Foreign Affairs*. Indianapolis, IN: Monaghan Press, 1945.

Moore, Samuel J.T. *Moore's Complete Civil War Guide to Richmond*. Richmond, VA: self-published, 1978.

Murfin, James. *The Gleam of Bayonets: The Battle of Antietam and the Maryland Campaign of 1862*. New York: Thomas Yoseloff, 1965.

Nevins, Allan, ed. *A Diary of Battle: Personal Journal of Colonel Charles S. Wainwright, 1861–1865*. New York: Harcourt Brace, 1962.

O'Connor, Robert. *The Man Who Could Might Have Saved the Union*. N.p., n.d.

One Hundred Fifty-Fifth Regimental Association. *Under the Maltese Ross, Antietam to Appomattox: Campaign of the One Hundred Fifty-Fifth Penna Regiment*. Pittsburgh, PA, 1910.

Otis, George W. *The Second Wisconsin Infantry*. Dayton, OH: Morningside Bookshop, 1984.

Pfanz, Donald C. *The Petersburg Campaign: Abraham Lincoln at City Point, March 20–April 9, 1865*. Lynchburg, VA: H.E. Howard, 1989.

Pickerall, W.N. *History of the Third Indiana Cavalry*. Indianapolis, IN, 1912.

Porter, David Dixon. *Incidents and Anecdotes of the Civil War*. New York: D. Appleton & Company, 1885.

Porter, Horace. "Campaigning with Grant." *Century Illustrated Monthly Magazine* 53, no. 28 (1896–97).

Powell, William H. *The Fifth Army Corps Army of the Potomac*. New York: G.P. Putnam's Sons, 1896.

Pryor, Sara R. *My Day: Reminiscences of a Long Life*. New York: Macmillan Company, 1909.

Pullen, John J. *The Twentieth Maine*. N.p.: Eyre & Spottiswoode, 1959.

Quaife, Milo M., ed. *From the Cannon's Mouth: The Civil War Letters of General A.S. Williams*. Detroit, MI: Wayne State University Press, 1959.

Reilly, O.T. *The Battlefield of Antietam*. Sharpsburg, MD: self-published, 1906.

Sandburg, Carl. *Abraham Lincoln: The War Years, 1861–1865*. 4 vols. New York: Harcourt Brace, 1939.

Schildt, John W. *Drums Along the Antietam*. Parsons, WV: McClain Print Company, 2004.

Sears, Stephen W. *Landscape Turned Red: The Battle of Antietam*. Norwalk, CT: Easton Press, 2004.

Sedgwick, John. *Correspondence of John Sedgwick, Major General*. 2 vols. New York: De Vinne Press, 1902–3.

Sheridan, Philip Henry. *Personal Memoirs of P.H. Sheridan*. 2 vols. New York: C.L. Webster, 1888.

Sherman, William Tecumseh. *Memoirs of General William T. Sherman*. 2 vols. New York: Appleton & Company, 1875.

Slocum, C.E. *The Life and Services of Major General Henry Warner Slocum*, Toledo, OH: Slocum Publishing Company, 1913.

Wells, Gideon, Secretary of the Navy, with Abraham Lincoln and Andrew Johnson. Diary. Houghton-Mifflin, 1909.

Worthington, Glenn H. *Fighting for Time: The Battle that Saved Washington*. Shippensburg, PA: White Mane Publishing Company, 1985.

INDEX

ABOUT THE AUTHOR

John W. Schildt grew up in Walkersville, Maryland, and is a graduate of Shepherd University and Wesley Theological Seminary. He has been a pastor, teacher and chaplain of the Twenty-Ninth Division Association. He is a founding member of the National Museum of Civil War Medicine in Frederick, Maryland, as well as the Save Historic Antietam Foundation. Among his many books are *Drums Along the Antietam*, *Roads to Gettysburg*, *These Honored Dead* and others. As a certified guide at Antietam, he has led tours of individuals, colleges, military groups and others for fifty years.

Visit us at
www.historypress.com